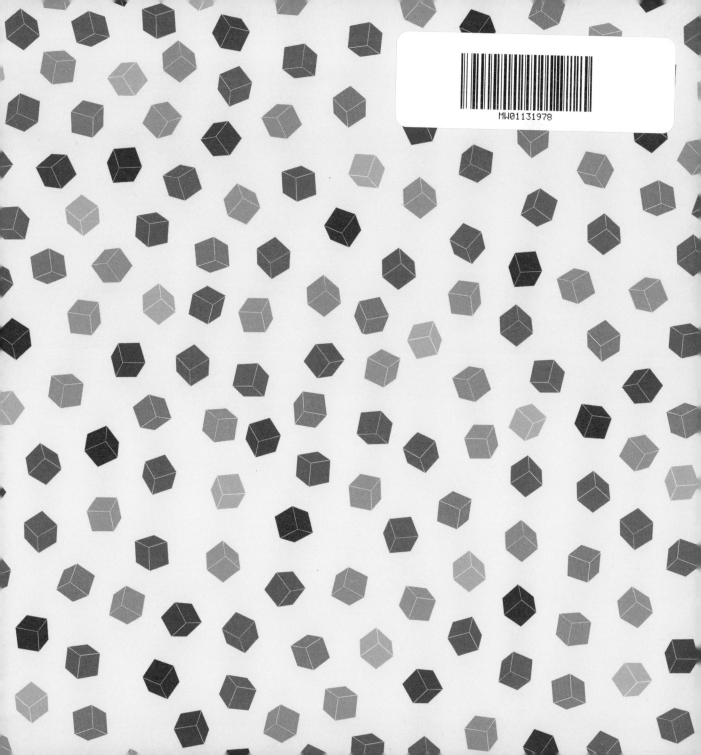

The EXTRAORDINARY ELEMENTS

For Finn and Zac – C.S.
For Maia and Nora – X.A.

BIG PICTURE PRESS

First published in the UK in 2020 by Big Picture Press,
an imprint of Bonnier Books UK,
The Plaza, 535 King's Road, London, SW10 0SZ
www.templarco.co.uk/big-picture-press
www.bonnierbooks.co.uk

ISBN 978-1-78741-734-2

This book was typeset in Ulissa and BSKombat.
The illustrations were created with graphite, wax and ink,
and coloured digitally.

Edited by Sophie Hallam and Joanna McInerney
Designed by Lee-May Lim, Edward Jennings and Adam Allori
Production Controller: Emma Kidd

Consultant: Nathan Adams

Printed in China

The
EXTRAORDINARY
ELEMENTS

Written by COLIN STUART

Illustrated by XIMO ABADÍA

B P P

CONTENTS

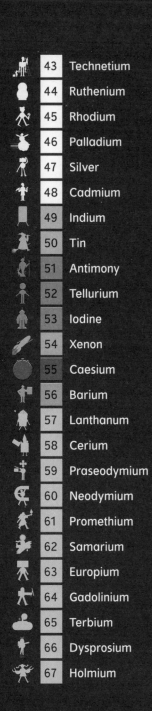

The Extraordinary Elements

Hold up your hand. What is it made of? Skin? Bone? But what are they made of?

Imagine using a microscope to zoom right down to scale ten million times smaller than a millimetre. If you could, you'd see that your hand – along with everything else in the Universe around us – is made of tiny building blocks called atoms. This book is your guide to this amazing atomic world.

In the middle of an **atom** you will find the **nucleus**. It is made of particles called **protons** and **neutrons**. Whizzing around this nucleus are **electrons**. Most of an atom is empty space – there's a large gap between the nucleus and the electrons. If you blew up an atom to the size of a city like London, UK then the nucleus would be about the size of a single person standing in the middle.

All atoms with an identical number of protons are given the same name. Gold, for example, has 79 protons. The oxygen you're breathing in right now has eight. These different materials are known as the **elements** and there are over one hundred of them. In the pages that follow you'll discover just how extraordinary these elements can be.

Chemistry is the study of the elements and the way they behave and interact with each other. A lot of chemistry boils down to the exact way electrons orbit the nucleus. They do this in layers called **shells**, which are bit like the orbits of planets around the Sun.

An element prefers to have full shells of electrons because it makes it more stable. So often it will try to borrow electrons if it needs more, or get rid of some if it has too many.

Elemental Basics

Elements are a bit like spies – each one has a secret code name. James Bond is famously 007. Similarly, chemists give special numbers to each element. The first is called the **atomic number** and is given the symbol Z. It counts the number of protons in the nucleus of that element. No two elements share the same atomic number – it's their unique signature. Chemists also talk about the **mass number** (given the symbol A). This is the total number of protons and neutrons added together.

Element	Symbol	Z	A
Nitrogen	N	7	14.007

Just like you can get different breeds of dogs or cats, it is possible to get different versions of the same element by adding extra neutrons. Take helium for example. Its atomic number is two because it always has two protons. But it can have anywhere between zero neutrons (helium-2) and eight neutrons (helium-10). The number after the element is the mass number.

Each element may be unique, but there are things that groups of elements have in common. Most are **solid** at normal room temperature (20°C). There are only twelve that are **gases** (hydrogen, helium, nitrogen, oxygen, fluorine, chlorine and the six noble gases). Just two elements – bromine and mercury – are **liquids**. Francium, caesium, gallium and rubidium will melt from solid to liquid if the temperature rises to 40°C.

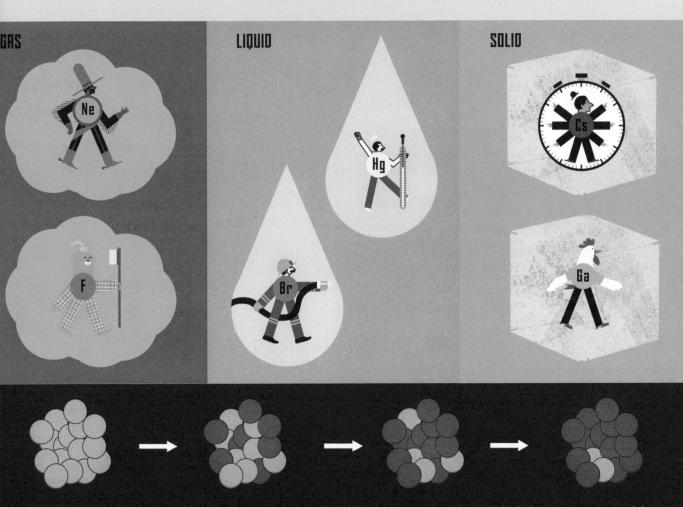

GAS

LIQUID

SOLID

The bigger an atom gets (the higher its mass number) the more unstable it becomes. Unstable atoms often break apart into smaller ones. This process is a called **radioactive decay** and all elements heavier than bismuth are radioactive. Imagine you had one hundred atoms of a radioactive element. The time it takes for half of them to decay is called the **half-life**. This can be incredibly quick – just a tiny fraction of a second – or many billions of years.

Chemistry 101

Elements crave stability. They can achieve this by acquiring a full outer shell of electrons. This can be done by filling up the outer shell with missing extra electrons or losing stray electrons so that the full shell beneath becomes the outermost. Atoms do this through a process called **bonding**. An **ionic bond** sees one atom donate electron(s) to another. **Covalent bonding** occurs when two or more atoms share electrons between them.

IONIC BONDING

COVALENT BONDING

Chemists write down a chemical reaction in the form of a **chemical equation**. An arrow separates the ingredients and the products and each chemical is separated with a plus sign. Chemicals that exist as molecules (two or more atoms joined together) have little numbers to tell you how many atoms they contain. H_2O for water is perhaps the most famous example – a water molecule has two atoms of hydrogen and one of oxygen.

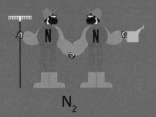

N_2

Na

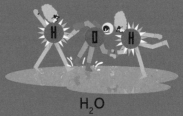

H_2O

Other symbols can help make it clear what is happening during a chemical reaction. Sometimes a reaction is reversible, meaning the products can turn back into the ingredients. This has a special double arrow symbol. Letters also symbolise the state a substance is in: (g) for gaseous, (s) for solid, (l) for liquid and (aq) for aqueous (meaning dissolved in water).

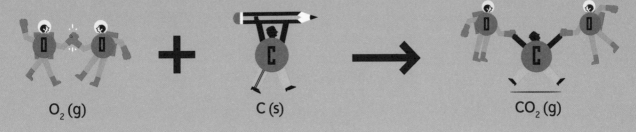

O_2 (g)   C (s) CO_2 (g)

Mass is always conserved during a chemical reaction. That means the total number of atoms that go into a reaction must equal the total number of atoms produced. So it is important to make sure the reaction you write down is balanced. This is done by adding numbers in front of each **chemical symbol** so that each side adds up to the same total.

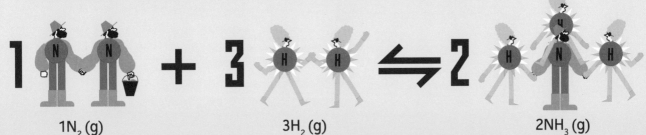

$1N_2$ (g) $3H_2$ (g) $2NH_3$ (g)   VI

How do we Discover the Elements?

There was a time when we thought that the Universe was made up of just four elements: air, water, earth and fire. Yet as we learned more we realised there was a better way to classify the ingredients that make up the world around us.

PREHISTORIC

The story starts thousands of years ago when our ancestors made use of new materials to build themselves a better world. The Iron Age started about 3,200 years ago and lasted for six hundred years. We learnt how to build tools out of the element with the atomic number 26. Iron is one of thirteen elements known to humans since ancient times. Others include gold, lead, tin and zinc.

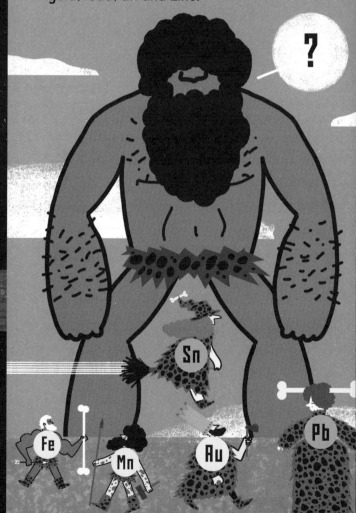

ALCHEMY

It was from the 1600s when the list really started to get bigger as scientists began to experiment with new **substances**. The element phosphorus was discovered in urine by an alchemist – a person trying to turn everyday **chemicals** into gold. By boiling chemicals and turning gases into liquids, alchemists identified a host of new elements including oxygen, nitrogen and hydrogen.

SPECTROSCOPY

The mid-1800s saw the rise of a technique called **spectroscopy**. Electrons moving between shells (see page XII) inside an atom give out light that is unique to that particular element. Scientists including Robert Bunsen – who gives his name to the Bunsen burner – used this light to discover elements caesium and rubidium.

During the 19th century there was a real explosion in the number of new elements discovered – a total of 49.

SYNTHETIC

A further 35 have been found since 1900. During and after World War Two, scientists were experimenting with **nuclear** weapons, such as atomic bombs. They discovered new elements including curium and americium while testing them. New elements were also found by firing small elements at bigger ones at really high speeds inside enormous machines – a method called **bombardment**. Mendelevium – named after the inventor of the **periodic table** (see p101) – was discovered in 1955 by firing helium at an element named after another famous scientist: einsteinium.

The Periodic Table

Our element story is far from finished – the number of elements is still growing as we work to discover new ones. That same bombardment technique is how the latest additions to the element list – tennessine and oganesson – were found in the twenty-first century. It is getting harder to find heavier elements because they are very unstable and disappear in the blink of an eye.

With well over one hundred elements to deal with, scientists organise them into groups based on the way they behave. It is called the **periodic table**, which was invented by Russian scientist Dmitri Mendeleev in 1869.

1 H Hydrogen												
3 Li Lithium	4 Be Beryllium											5
11 Na Sodium	12 Mg Magnesium											13
19 K Potassium	20 Ca Calcium	21 Sc Scandium	22 Ti Titanium	23 V Vanadium	24 Cr Chromium	25 Mn Manganese	26 Fe Iron	27 Co Cobalt	28 Ni Nickel	29 Cu Copper	30 Zn Zinc	31 G
37 Rb Rubidium	38 Sr Strontium	39 Y Yttrium	40 Zr Zirconium	41 Nb Niobium	42 Mo Molybdenum	43 Tc Technetium	44 Ru Ruthenium	45 Rh Rhodium	46 Pd Palladium	47 Ag Silver	48 Cd Cadmium	49 I
55 Cs Caesium	56 Ba Barium	57–71 ▼	72 Hf Hafnium	73 Ta Tantalum	74 W Tungsten	75 Re Rhenium	76 Os Osmium	77 Ir Iridium	78 Pt Platinum	79 Au Gold	80 Hg Mercury	81 Th
87 Fr Francium	87 Ra Radium	89–103 ▼	104 Rf Rutherfordium	105 Db Dubnium	106 Sg Seaborgium	107 Bh Bohrium	108 Hs Hassium	109 Mt Meitnerium	110 Ds Darmstadtium	111 Rg Roentgenium	112 Cn Copernicium	11 N

Lanthanides	57 La Lanthanum	58 Ce Cerium	59 Pr Praseodymium	60 Nd Neodymium	61 Pm Promethium	62 Sm Samarium	63 Eu Europium	64 Gd Gadolinium	65 Tb Terbium	66 Dy Dysprosium	67 H Ho
Actinides	89 Ac Actinium	90 Th Thorium	91 Pa Protactinium	92 U Uranium	93 Np Neptunium	94 Pu Plutonium	95 Am Americium	96 Cm Curium	97 Bk Berkelium	98 Cf Californium	99 Eins

The rows are called **'periods'**, which is where the name of the table comes from. Elements get heavier as you move from left to right along a period. The size of an atom of each element decreases from left to right because adding more protons means the nucleus can keep electrons in a tighter orbit around it.

The table has eighteen columns called **'groups'**. Normally all elements in a group have a similar pattern of electrons in their outer shell. Elements get heavier as you move down a group.

| He |
| Ne |
| Ar |
| Kr |
| Xe |
| Rn |
| Og |

| K | Ca | Sc | Ti | V | Cr | Mn | Fe | Co | Ni | Cu | Zn | Ga | Ge | As | Se | Br | Kr |

			2 **He** Helium
7 **N** Nitrogen	8 **O** Oxygen	9 **F** Flourine	10 **Ne** Neon
15 **P** Phosphorus	16 **S** Sulfur	17 **Cl** Chlorine	18 **Ar** Argon
33 **As** Arsenic	34 **Se** Selenium	35 **Br** Bromine	36 **Kr** Krypton
51 **Sb** Antimony	52 **Te** Tellurium	53 **I** Iodine	54 **Xe** Xenon
83 **Bi** Bismuth	84 **Po** Polonium	85 **At** Astantine	86 **Rn** Radon
115 **Mc** Moscovium	116 **Lv** Livermorium	117 **Ts** Tennessine	118 **Og** Oganesson

| 69 **Tm** Thulium | 70 **Yb** Ytterbium | 71 **Lu** Lutetium |
| 101 **Md** Mendelevium | 102 **No** Nobelium | 103 **Lr** Lawrencium |

To save more space, elements are given a one or two letter **symbol**. It could be its first letter – such as C for carbon and O for oxygen, or based on the Latin name for the element like Pb for lead (plumbum).

6 **C** Carbon

There are so many elements in two periods – the lanthanides and actinides – that they are moved to the bottom to stop the table becoming too wide. That makes it easier to print in books like this one. The lanthanides and actinides are just two examples of other ways to group the elements (see the colour-coded sets on pXI).

Key

Every time a new element is discovered it gets added to the periodic table. Chemists know exactly where to put it because it runs from the element with the lowest atomic number (hydrogen) to the highest (currently oganesson). Its inventor – Dmitri Mendeleev – even left gaps for elements yet to be discovered. What makes the periodic table such a smart tool is that elements that behave similarly appear close together. These groups are colour-coded, as you will see below.

ALKALI METALS
The first column of the periodic table is home to the alkali metals (hydrogen doesn't belong to this group). The alkali metals are shiny, highly reactive and soft enough to cut with a knife.

ALKALI EARTH METALS
The six silvery-white elements in Group 2 have low melting and boiling points. They often form **compounds** with the halogens, including sodium chloride (also known as table salt).

TRANSITION METALS
This is by far the biggest group in the table with 35 members – that's almost a third of all known elements. Transition metals are very hard, with high melting points and boiling points.

POST-TRANSITION METALS
The post-transition metals usually prefer to bond with other elements using covalent bonds. There is a lot of debate among chemists as to which elements to include in this group.

METALLOIDS
The behaviour of a metalloid is a cross between a metal and a non-metal. Their appearance is similar to metals, but they are not good conductors of electricity.

NON-METALS
Non-metals are usually light and poo[r] conductors of heat and electricity. Many o[f] them play a key role in biology.

HALOGENS
These elements make up a small group of five non-metals that often combine with metals to make salts. They are often used as disinfectants

THE NOBLE GASES
The noble gases already have a full outer shell of electrons so they tend not to get involved in chemical reactions. Usually they don't have a smell or colour either.

LANTHANIDES
These are named after the first element in the group (lanthanum). Along with scandium and yttrium they make up another class called the Rare Earth elements because they tend to be dug out of the Earth's crust.

ACTINIDES
Unlike most clusters in the periodic table, the properties of the actinides vary considerably across its fifteen metallic elements. All actinide[s] are radioactive.

A Guide to the Elements

Each element in this book will be assigned symbols to tell you more about it.

STATE AT 20°C

These symbols inidcate the state of each element at 20°C (solid, liquid or gas).

WHERE ON EARTH?

This symbol indicates where you can find the element in the world.

DANGER TO LIFE

This indicates whether a substance is non-toxic, toxic or a mixture.

SPECIAL USES

This highlights how we make use of the element to improve our lives.

DATE OF DISCOVERY

A magnifying glass indicates the year the element was 'discovered'. Often, this indicates the date it was first isolated.

ELEMENT RANKINGS

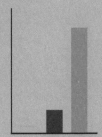

Every element has a different **density**, **melting point** and **boiling point**. In the pages that follow, every element has been ranked from 1 to 118 from highest to lowest for each of these three key properties. A category plot like the one shown here will illustrate this information on each page.

ELECTRON SHELL CONFIGURATION

Below, you can see an example of an element's electron shell configuration. The electrons whizzing around the nucleus determine the element's chemical properties – the way it behaves in a chemical reaction. The total number of electron shells an atom has determines what period the element is in. The number of electrons in its outermost shell determines the group. The number in the middle represents the protons in the nucleus of that element – its unique signature.

ATOMIC MASS
83.798

This number indicates the average mass of an element's **isotopes** as found in nature.

This circle fills as the atomic number increases.

These bars indicate which row the element can be found on.

This number indicates the atomic number of the element, and is also the page number.

HYDROGEN

ELECTRON CONFIGURATION

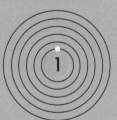

1

ATOMIC MASS
1.008

ELEMENT RANKINGS

118

2
2
1

MELTING POINT | BOILING POINT | DENSITY

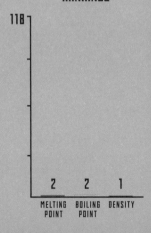

STATE AT 20°C
A colourless, odourless gas.

WHERE ON EARTH?
Found in the greatest quantities as water.

DANGER TO LIFE
Non-toxic, it is essential for almost all living things.

SPECIAL USES
Clean fuel, fertiliser, margarine, silicon chips.

A FUTURE FUEL

DISCOVERED IN 1766

Hydrogen is the oldest and most abundant element. It makes up 75 per cent of the Universe and provides the fuel for stars. Hydrogen is also the simplest element with a solitary electron orbiting one proton, making it so light that it can easily escape Earth's gravity. Hydrogen is also the main constituent of water (H_2O) and extracting it from water could give us a clean energy source as we try and move away from fossil fuels.

HELIUM

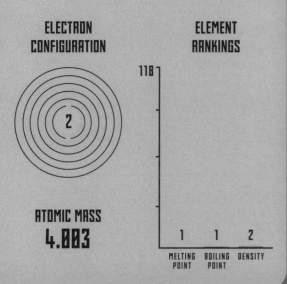

ELECTRON CONFIGURATION

2

ELEMENT RANKINGS

118

1	1	2
MELTING POINT	BOILING POINT	DENSITY

ATOMIC MASS
4.003

STATE AT 20°C
A colourless, odourless gas.

WHERE ON EARTH?
Found in natural gas which contains up to 7% helium.

DANGER TO LIFE
No known biological role. It is non-toxic.

SPECIAL USES
MRI scanners, supermarket scanners, deep-sea divers.

SHORT SUPPLY

 DISCOVERED IN 1895

First discovered on the Sun, helium is named after Helius, the Greek sun god. Whilst it is the second most abundant element in the Universe, you can't just grab hold of it on Earth. Helium is mostly produced as a by-product of the natural gas industry and is now in short supply. As it's lighter than air, it's commonly used in zeppelins and party balloons. But think twice before your next birthday, as helium supplies are running out and we need it for important medical equipment.

LITHIUM

STATE AT 20°C
A soft, silvery metal.

WHERE ON EARTH?
Found in igneous rocks, seawater and mineral springs.

DANGER TO LIFE
No known biological role. It is toxic, except in small doses.

SPECIAL USES
Toys, clocks, aircraft, bicycle frames, high-speed trains.

A BIG BANG

 DISCOVERED IN 1817

Lithium is the only metal light enough to float on water. It is so reactive that it is rare to find on Earth on its own – normally it has combined with other elements to form a compound. It was one of the elements made in the first minutes after the birth of our Universe during the Big Bang. Today, it is used to create red colours in fireworks displays. More commonly, we use it to make the small but powerful batteries found in devices such as smartphones. Lithium was famously the title of a popular track by the rock band Nirvana.

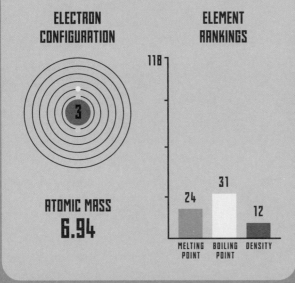

ELECTRON CONFIGURATION

3

ATOMIC MASS
6.94

ELEMENT RANKINGS

118

MELTING POINT	BOILING POINT	DENSITY
24	31	12

BERYLLIUM

Be

ELECTRON CONFIGURATION

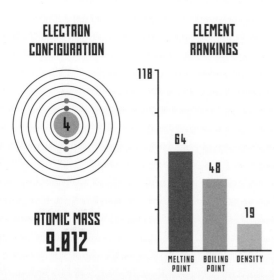

4

ATOMIC MASS
9.012

ELEMENT RANKINGS

118

64 — MELTING POINT
48 — BOILING POINT
19 — DENSITY

STATE AT 20°C
A soft, silvery-white metal.

WHERE ON EARTH?
Found in 30 different mineral species including emerald.

DANGER TO LIFE
Deadly poisonous if dust or fumes are inhaled.

SPECIAL USES
Gyroscopes, springs, high-speed aircraft, X-rays.

COSMIC RAIN

 DISCOVERED IN 1797

Gemstones containing the mineral beryl, such as emeralds, have been known since ancient times. When chemists later isolated the main element inside, they called it beryllium. It is mostly made when high-energy particles called cosmic rays strike the Earth's atmosphere from space. This creates a shower of particles – including beryllium – which rain down from the sky. Its properties make it perfect for spacecraft and communication satellites.

BORON

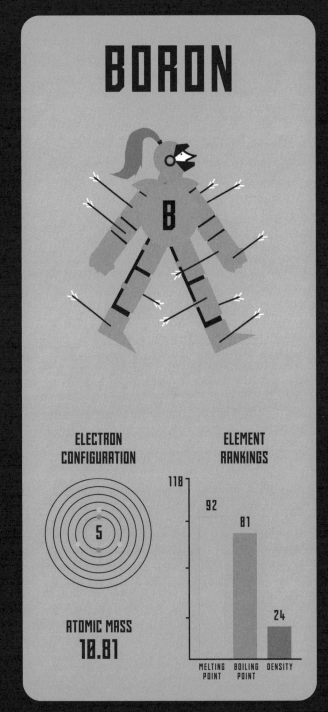

B

ELECTRON CONFIGURATION

5

ATOMIC MASS
10.81

ELEMENT RANKINGS

118

92 — MELTING POINT
81 — BOILING POINT
24 — DENSITY

STATE AT 20°C
A dark, black-brown powder in its purest state.

WHERE ON EARTH?
Found in volcanic spring waters and in minerals such as borax.

DANGER TO LIFE
It is non-toxic but can upset the body's metabolism if consumed.

SPECIAL USES
Rocket fuel igniter, pyrotechnic flares, washing powders.

HARD STUFF
DISCOVERED IN 1808

The name boron comes from the Persian or Arabic terms for the mineral borax (*burah* or *buraq*). Borax and boric acid have been known since ancient times in Europe, Tibet and China. They were used by craftsmen to reduce the melting point of materials in glassmaking and other applications. Today, boron carbide (B_4C) is used in armour plating for vehicles and bulletproof vests. It has also been found on the Moon and Mars, and in some meteorites.

CARBON

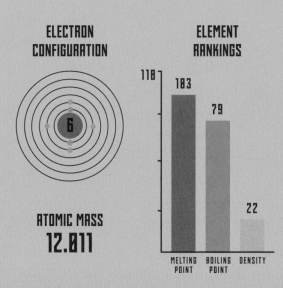

STATE AT 20°C
Found in many forms: graphite, diamond, graphene.

WHERE ON EARTH?
Found in the Sun, the stars and in our atmosphere.

DANGER TO LIFE
Non-toxic, it is essential for all living things.

SPECIAL USES
Tennis rackets, skis, fishing rods, rockets, aeroplanes.

LIFE ON EARTH
 DISCOVERED IN ANCIENT TIMES

Carbon is the basis for life on Earth. It is unique in its ability to form complex chemicals by bonding with other elements in a variety of ways including single, double and triple bonds. The 'lead' in a pencil isn't lead at all, but graphite – a material made from carbon atoms arranged in hexagons. Diamond may look very different but it is also made of carbon. And it's not just the hard stuff, almost everything you eat is made up from carbon compounds, too.

ELECTRON CONFIGURATION

6

ATOMIC MASS
12.011

ELEMENT RANKINGS

118

103
MELTING POINT

79
BOILING POINT

22
DENSITY

NITROGEN

STATE AT 20°C
A colourless, odourless gas.

WHERE ON EARTH?
Found in all living things, it makes up 78% of the air, by volume.

DANGER TO LIFE
Non-toxic, it is essential for all living things.

SPECIAL USES
Dyes, explosives, freezing food, fertilisers, nitric acid, nylon.

KEY INGREDIENT
DISCOVERED IN 1772

Nitrogen is the most abundant element in the Earth's atmosphere, making up 78 per cent of the air we breathe. It is also a key ingredient for life, found in important biological chemicals such as amino acids. Compounds of nitrogen – called nitrates – are a crucial part of the fertilisers used by farmers and gardeners to help grow plants. Super cold liquid nitrogen can be used by chefs to help make cold food such as ice-creams and sorbets.

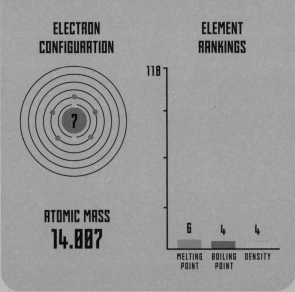

ELECTRON CONFIGURATION

7

ATOMIC MASS
14.007

ELEMENT RANKINGS

118

MELTING POINT	BOILING POINT	DENSITY
6	4	4

OXYGEN

STATE AT 20°C
A colourless, odourless gas.

WHERE ON EARTH?
Found in the atmosphere, the Earth's crust and the human body.

DANGER TO LIFE
Non-toxic, it is essential for all living things.

SPECIAL USES
Steel industry, anti-freeze, polyester.

3-MINUTE RULE

DISCOVERED IN 1774

Oxygen is arguably the most important element to you. You cannot last more than three minutes without it. Although it is the third most abundant element in the Universe, and makes up 21 percent of Earth's atmosphere, astronauts still need spacesuits to make sure they have an oxygen supply in space. It is the most reactive of all the non-metals, so easily bonds with other elements to form compounds such as water (H_2O), carbon dioxide (CO_2) and iron oxide (rust, Fe_2O_3).

ELECTRON CONFIGURATION

ELEMENT RANKINGS

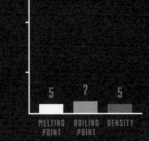

118

5	7	5
MELTING POINT	BOILING POINT	DENSITY

ATOMIC MASS
15.999

FLUORINE

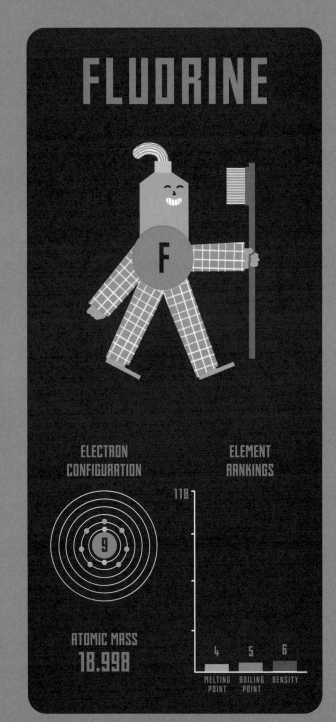

STATE AT 20°C
A pale yellow-green gas.

WHERE ON EARTH?
Found in the minerals fluorite, fluorspar and cryolite.

DANGER TO LIFE
Essential to humans, (our bodies contains about 3mg) but highly toxic in pure form.

SPECIAL USES
Nuclear energy, frosting glass, light bulbs.

ELECTRON CONFIGURATION

9

ATOMIC MASS
18.998

ELEMENT RANKINGS

118

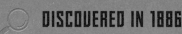

	4	5	6
	MELTING POINT	BOILING POINT	DENSITY

PEARLY WHITES

DISCOVERED IN 1886

Despite its common usage in toothpaste, fluorine is the most chemically reactive element. Fluorine reacts, often very vigorously, with all of the other elements except oxygen, helium, neon and krypton. Fluorine is also the most electronegative element. In molecules, this means that fluorine attracts electrons more powerfully than any other element. It is often added to tap water to help fight tooth decay but too much fluoride is toxic.

NEON

STATE AT 20°C
A colourless, odourless, tasteless gas.

WHERE ON EARTH?
Found in Earth's atmosphere, it is the 5th most abundant element.

DANGER TO LIFE
No known biological role. It is non-toxic.

SPECIAL USES
Neon signs, diving equipment, high-voltage indicators, lasers.

VIVA LAS VEGAS

 DISCOVERED IN 1898

Neon is associated with bright signs that glow vibrant red-orange, famous in Las Vegas, USA. As the second lightest noble gas, neon doesn't usually take part in chemical reactions. Yet if you pass an electric current through a tube of neon it boosts electrons into higher shells. When they fall back down again they give off a distinctive colour, which one of neon's discovererers – William Ramsay – referred to as a 'brilliant flame-covered light' in his Nobel Prize speech.

ELECTRON CONFIGURATION

ELEMENT RANKINGS

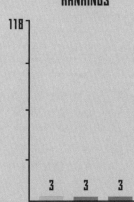

118

	MELTING POINT	BOILING POINT	DENSITY
	3	3	3

ATOMIC MASS
20.18

SODIUM

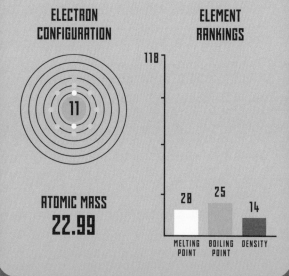

STATE AT 20°C
A soft metal that tarnishes quickly in air.

WHERE ON EARTH?
Found in salt beds and minerals such as sodalite and cryolite.

DANGER TO LIFE
Sodium compounds are vital to life, but pure sodium is highly dangerous

SPECIAL USES
Nuclear reactors, common salt, de-icer, water softener.

A BIT OF SALT

DISCOVERED IN 1807

Soft enough to be cut with a knife, sodium belongs to the alkali metal family. We use it a lot in our everyday life: to season our food in the form of sodium chloride (table salt) or sodium bicarbonate (baking powder) in cooking. Our bodies use sodium for lots of different things, such as sending signals between nerve cells. Our street lights are gradually switching to LED bulbs, but some still use sodium to create light in a similar way to neon signs.

ELECTRON CONFIGURATION

11

ATOMIC MASS
22.99

ELEMENT RANKINGS

118

MELTING POINT	BOILING POINT	DENSITY
20	25	14

MAGNESIUM

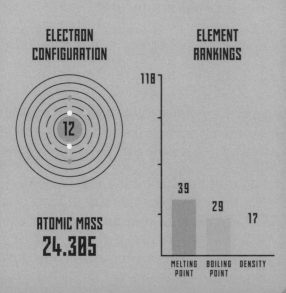

STATE AT 20°C
A silvery-white metal that burns with a bright light.

WHERE ON EARTH?
Found in the sea and in minerals such as magnesite and dolomite.

DANGER TO LIFE
Non-toxic, it is essential in both plant and animal life.

SPECIAL USES
Car seats, laptops, cameras, power tools, cattle feed.

ELECTRON CONFIGURATION

12

ATOMIC MASS
24.305

ELEMENT RANKINGS

110

39

29

17

MELTING POINT | BOILING POINT | DENSITY

GREEN AS GRASS

DISCOVERED IN 1755

Difficult to extinguish because of its ability to burn with nitrogen, water and carbon dioxide, this shiny metallic element produces bright flames. That's why it is often used in fireworks and sparklers. A single ion of magnesium is also found in the centre of chlorophyll cells – the green pigment that gives plants their colour. It plays a crucial role in photosynthesis – the process by which plants create their own food by turning sunlight and carbon dioxide into sugar and oxygen.

ALUMINIUM

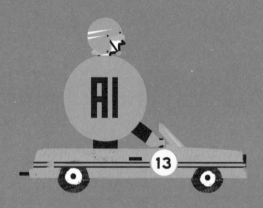

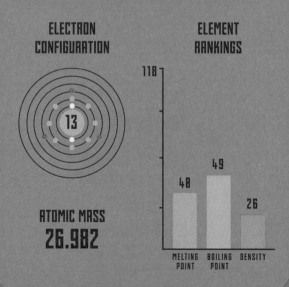

13

ELECTRON CONFIGURATION

13

ATOMIC MASS
26.982

ELEMENT RANKINGS

118

48
49
26

MELTING POINT | BOILING POINT | DENSITY

STATE AT 20°C
A silvery-white, lightweight metal.

WHERE ON EARTH?
Found in minerals such as bauxite and cryolite.

DANGER TO LIFE
No known biological role on Earth. It can be toxic if inhaled in high concentrations.

SPECIAL USES
Aeroplane parts, telescope mirrors, decorative paper, toys.

SHINE ON

DISCOVERED IN 1825

Today we use this lightweight, strong and non-corrosive metal for everything from cars, cans and kitchen foil to painting the white lines on tennis courts. You'll even find it in sun cream. In fact, there's only one metallic element – iron – that we use more than aluminium. We've been using it for millennia, too. Back in Ancient Greece and Rome it was used in dyes and for dressing wounds. It is good at fighting the microbes that cause some diseases.

SILICON

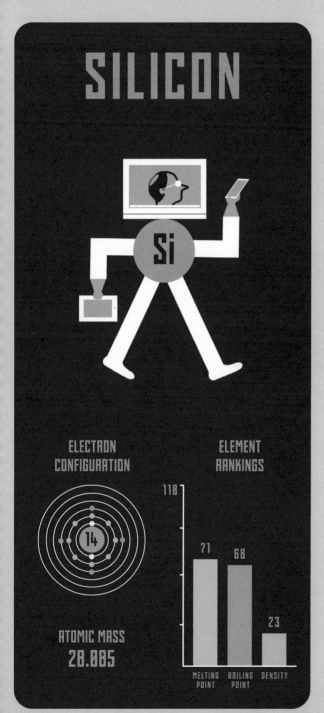

ELECTRON
CONFIGURATION

14

ATOMIC MASS
28.085

ELEMENT
RANKINGS

118

71   68

23

MELTING   BOILING   DENSITY
POINT   POINT

STATE AT 20°C
A blue-grey metallic sheen
in its purest state.

WHERE ON EARTH?
Found in sand and minerals. It is
the 2nd most abundant element.

DANGER TO LIFE
Essential to plants. It is non-toxic
but can be carcinogenic if silicates
are inhaled.

SPECIAL USES
Fibre optics, cosmetics,
hair conditioner, concrete.

SUPER SAVVY

 DISCOVERED IN 1824

Silicon is the base for a lot of our
computer technology. Computer
chips are usually made of this hard,
unreactive element. Silicon was chosen
because there's a lot of it (it makes up
over 25% of the Earth's crust and is
a major component of sand) but also
its electrical properties are part-way
between a conductor and an insulator.
There's even an area of California,
USA named Silicon Valley due to the
large number of technology companies
based there.

PHOSPHORUS

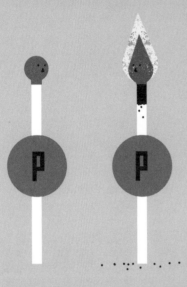

ELECTRON CONFIGURATION

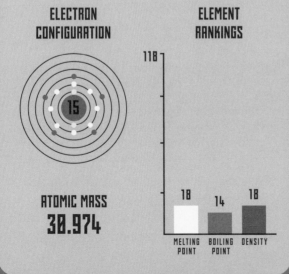

15

ATOMIC MASS
30.974

ELEMENT RANKINGS

MELTING POINT	BOILING POINT	DENSITY
18	14	18

118

STATE AT 20°C
A poisonous, waxy solid (white) or a non-toxic solid (red).

WHERE ON EARTH?
Found in minerals such as phosphate rock (but it is running out).

DANGER TO LIFE
Essential to all living things (our bodies contain about 750g), but it is highly toxic in pure form.

SPECIAL USES
Flares, matchboxes, fertilisers, steel, fine chinaware.

COLD FIRE
DISCOVERED IN 1669

Originally known as 'cold fire' because it glows in the dark, phosphorus gets its name from the Greek word *phosphoros*, meaning 'bringer of light'. It's still used in the heads of matches because of this. It was difficult to discover because it ignites spontaneously in air. Phosphorus is also found in human DNA and is a key ingredient in many fertilisers. People were so desperate for phosphorous in the 1800s that they extracted it from bird and bat poo.

SULFUR

ELECTRON CONFIGURATION

16

ELEMENT RANKINGS

118

22
MELTING POINT

17
BOILING POINT

21
DENSITY

ATOMIC MASS
32.06

STATE AT 20°C
A yellow crystal or powder.

WHERE ON EARTH?
Found in many minerals such as gypsum and in volcanic areas.

DANGER TO LIFE
Essential to all living things (our bodies contain about 140g), but can cause skin irritation.

SPECIAL USES
Black rubber, black gunpowder, silver polish, bleach, cement.

ROTTEN EGGS

 DISCOVERED IN ANCIENT TIMES

Chances are you've already smelled sulfur. Many of its compounds stink, including hydrogen sulfide (H_2S) which smells like rotten eggs. Sulfur has been known for most of human history and was regarded by alchemists as one of three substances that make up everything in the Universe. It is one of the oldest fungicides and pesticides, used for centuries to protect crops from other harmful living things. Despite that destructive ability, it also plays a crucial role in your body.

CHLORINE

ELECTRON CONFIGURATION

17

ATOMIC MASS
35.45

ELEMENT RANKINGS

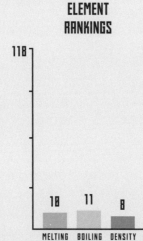

118

10	11	8
MELTING POINT	BOILING POINT	DENSITY

STATE AT 20°C
A yellowy-green dense gas with a distinctive smell.

WHERE ON EARTH?
Largely produced from the compound sodium chloride.

DANGER TO LIFE
Essential to all living things but can be highly toxic.

SPECIAL USES
Disinfectant, paper, paints, textiles, insecticides, PVC.

GERM KILLER

DISCOVERED IN 1774

Widely associated with the smell of swimming pools, chlorine is often used as a cleaning product to kill bacteria. In its standard state, the yellow-coloured chlorine gas is highly toxic to humans. Yet you'll still find it in your stomach combined with hydrogen to form hydrochloric acid (HCl). This acid helps to break down the food that you eat. Chlorine gas is very poisonous, and was used as a chemical weapon during World War I.

ARGON

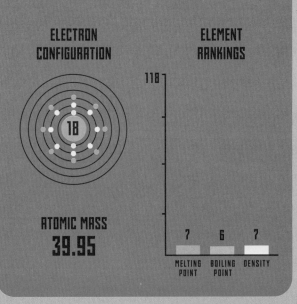

Ar

ELECTRON CONFIGURATION

18

ELEMENT RANKINGS

118

	7	6	7
	MELTING POINT	BOILING POINT	DENSITY

ATOMIC MASS
39.95

STATE AT 20°C
A colourless, odourless gas.

WHERE ON EARTH?
Found in 0.94% of the Earth's atmosphere.

DANGER TO LIFE
No known biological role. It is non-toxic.

SPECIAL USES
Low-energy light bulbs, tyres, food and drink containers.

THE LAZY ONE

 DISCOVERED IN 1894

The first noble gas to be discovered, argon is named the 'lazy one' due to its incredibly unreactive nature. This property means that it is often used to replace oxygen inside food and drink containers so that the contents last longer. Despite this lack of reactivity, argon produces a beautiful blue-purple hue when stimulated by electricity and is widely used for both incandescent and fluorescent lighting. It is the third most abundant gas in the Earth's atmosphere after nitrogen and oxygen.

POTASSIUM

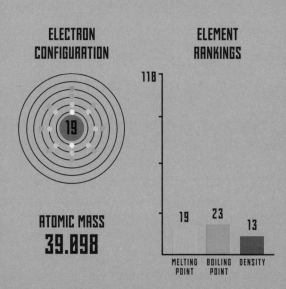

STATE AT 20°C
A soft, silvery-white metal that tarnishes quickly in air.

WHERE ON EARTH?
Found in the ocean, igneous rocks and minerals such as sylvite.

DANGER TO LIFE
Essential to all living things as a compound (our bodies contain about 140g), but dangerous in pure form.

SPECIAL USES
Fertilisers, glass, detergent, liquid soap, pharmaceuticals.

COOL BANANA

 DISCOVERED IN 1807

Potassium is vital to life and is found in many areas of the human body, from controlling your blood pressure to breaking down food. It is therefore important to consume potassium as part of a healthy diet, with bananas and fish being good examples of potassium-rich foods. As well as being good for the body, it is the basis for some deadly poisons such as cyanide. Potassium nitrate is also used in fireworks and gunpowder.

ELECTRON CONFIGURATION

19

ATOMIC MASS
39.098

ELEMENT RANKINGS

110

MELTING POINT 19
BOILING POINT 23
DENSITY 13

CALCIUM

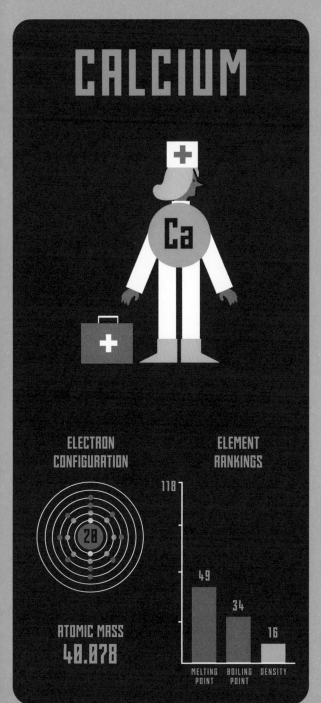

Ca

ELECTRON
CONFIGURATION

20

ATOMIC MASS
40.078

ELEMENT
RANKINGS

118

49
34
16

MELTING
POINT | BOILING
POINT | DENSITY

STATE AT 20°C
A soft, silvery-white metal that tarnishes quickly in air.

WHERE ON EARTH?
Found in limestone, gypsum, fluorite and apatite.

DANGER TO LIFE
Essential to all living things (our bodies contain about 1kg), but dangerous in pure form when exposed to water.

SPECIAL USES
Building stone, cement, soil conditioner, anti-freeze agent.

ALL BONES
DISCOVERED IN 1808

Abundant on both the Earth and the Moon, calcium is essential for animal and plant nutrition and is vital for building strong bones and teeth. Good sources of calcium include milk, cheese and yoghurt, although too much calcium can cause kidney stones. Medics use calcium sulfate as plaster for setting bones. Calcium is also a key ingredient in steel making and car batteries and can be found in chalk and limestone (both forms of calcium carbonate).

SCANDIUM

Sc

STATE AT 20°C
A silvery metal that tarnishes in air, burns easily and reacts with water.

WHERE ON EARTH?
Found in small quantities in over 800 mineral species.

DANGER TO LIFE
No known biological role. A suspected carcinogen and flammable in pure form.

SPECIAL USES
Fighter planes, television cameras, research.

POWER HITTER

DISCOVERED BY 1879

Named after Scandinavia, scandium alloys are often used in sports equipment including baseball bats and bicycle frames to lighten the weight, increase strength and because of its resistance to corrosion. Those same properties mean that it is also used in building aircraft, particularly for the military. Not that it comes cheap – scandium is one the most expensive elements to buy. It was one of the missing elements predicted by Dmitri Mendeleev when he invented the periodic table.

ELECTRON CONFIGURATION

ELEMENT RANKINGS

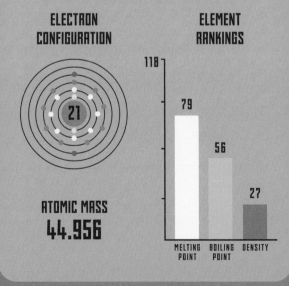

21

ATOMIC MASS
44.956

118

79	56	27
MELTING POINT	BOILING POINT	DENSITY

TITANIUM

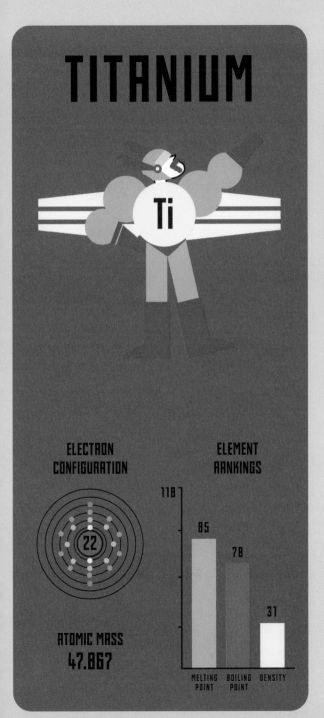

Ti

ELECTRON CONFIGURATION

22

ATOMIC MASS
47.867

ELEMENT RANKINGS

118

85
78
31

MELTING POINT | BOILING POINT | DENSITY

STATE AT 20°C
A hard, shiny and strong metal

WHERE ON EARTH?
Found in igneous rocks, iron ores and in minerals such as ilmenite.

DANGER TO LIFE
No known biological role.
It is non-toxic.

SPECIAL USES
Laptops, bicycles, fishing rods, plastics, sunscreens.

FIRE AWAY

DISCOVERED IN 1791

Super-strength titanium is named after the Titans in Greek mythology, a group of powerful gods and goddesses. This transition metal is both strong and lightweight and makes alloys which are ideal for aircraft, spacecraft, missiles and ships. It is also an ideal choice for new body parts and is widely used in hip and knee replacements, as well as dental implants. Titanium dioxide is this element's most common compound, used as a white paint and in golf clubs.

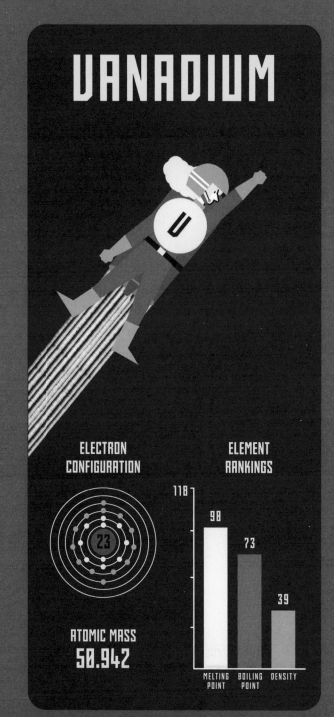

VANADIUM

ELECTRON CONFIGURATION

23

ATOMIC MASS
50.942

ELEMENT RANKINGS

118

90

73

39

MELTING POINT | BOILING POINT | DENSITY

STATE AT 20°C
A silvery-grey metal that resists corrosion.

WHERE ON EARTH?
Found in about 65 different minerals including vanadinite.

DANGER TO LIFE
Essential to humans; but our bodies only need 0.01 milligrams each day.

SPECIAL USES
Armour plates, axles, tools, piston rods, glass, magnets.

UP, UP & AWAY

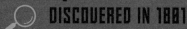

DISCOVERED IN 1801

When vanadium was first discovered, the original sample and findings were lost in a shipwreck. It took three decades to find this elusive element again and it was eventually named after Vanadís, the Swedish goddess of beauty. Today this silvery-grey metal is used in industry to improve the strength of steel and to create a special alloy that is a key component in jet engines. Enzymes containing vanadium are even used by some sea algae during photosynthesis to remove unwanted chemicals.

CHROMIUM

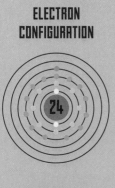

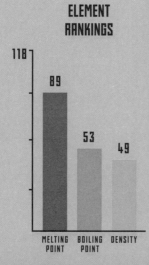

ELECTRON CONFIGURATION

24

ATOMIC MASS
51.996

ELEMENT RANKINGS

110

89

53

49

MELTING POINT

BOILING POINT

DENSITY

STATE AT 20°C
A hard, silvery metal with a blue tinge.

WHERE ON EARTH?
Found mainly in the ore chromite.

DANGER TO LIFE
Essential to humans (our bodies only need 1mg each day), but highly toxic as a compound.

SPECIAL USES
Stainless steel, chromium plating, tanning leather.

ALL RAINBOW

 DISCOVERED IN 1798

Named after the Greek word for colour (chroma), chromium produces the beautiful colours seen in precious gems from red rubies to green emeralds. Chromium compounds also come in a rainbow of colours and are often used in paints and lasers. However, this element is mostly used to create strong alloys. For example, it is found in stainless steel cutlery. Our ancient ancestors used to coat the tips of swords with chromium to stop them corroding.

MANGANESE

STATE AT 20°C
A silvery-grey metal.

WHERE ON EARTH?
Found on the ocean floor and in minerals such as pyrolusite.

DANGER TO LIFE
Essential to all living things (our bodies contain about 12mg), but highly reactive with water.

SPECIAL USES
Alloys, safes, prison bars, drinks cans, fertilisers, ceramics.

CAVE MAN

 DISCOVERED IN 1774

Manganese is a silvery-grey, hard and very brittle metal similar to its neighbour, iron. Unlike iron it is not magnetic. Yet another important component of steel, manganese is also vital for animal growth and plays a big role in bone formation. It is used as a pigment and there is evidence of humans using manganese as far back as 30,000 years ago to create sprawling paintings on cave walls. Manganese takes its name from Magnesia, a region of Greece.

ELECTRON CONFIGURATION

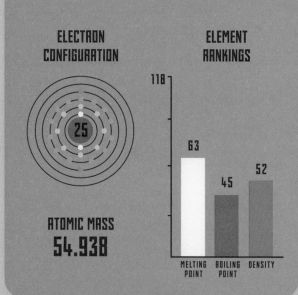

25

ATOMIC MASS
54.938

ELEMENT RANKINGS

118

63
45
52

MELTING POINT | BOILING POINT | DENSITY

IRON

Fe

ELECTRON CONFIGURATION

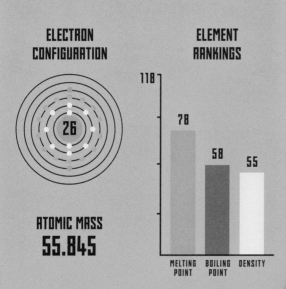

26

ATOMIC MASS
55.845

ELEMENT RANKINGS

118

78

58

55

MELTING POINT | BOILING POINT | DENSITY

STATE AT 20°C
A shiny, greyish metal that rusts in damp air.

WHERE ON EARTH?
Found in the ore haematite and minerals such as magnetite.

DANGER TO LIFE
Essential to all living things (our bodies contain about 4g) but toxic in large amounts (over 21g).

SPECIAL USES
Steel, bridges, electricity pylons, bicycle chains, jewellery.

PUMPING IRON

 DISCOVERED IN ANCIENT TIMES

As the major component of Earth's core, and one of the most common elements of the crust, iron has been used since ancient times. It gives its name to the Iron Age, a time when it was widely used to make tools. When alloyed to make steel, it is 1,000 times stronger than iron alone. Iron is also essential for life and is a key component in the red blood cells that carry oxygen around your body. However, it can cause poisoning if consumed in high dosages.

COBALT

Co

ELECTRON CONFIGURATION

27

ELEMENT RANKINGS

118

74

61

62

| MELTING POINT | BOILING POINT | DENSITY |

ATOMIC MASS
58.933

STATE AT 20°C
A magnetic, silvery-blue metal.

WHERE ON EARTH?
Found in the minerals cobaltite, skutterudite and erythrite.

DANGER TO LIFE
Essential to all living things (our bodies contain about 1mg) but toxic in large amounts (over 20g).

SPECIAL USES
Magnets, jet turbines, porcelain, glass, pottery, enamels.

GREEN GOBLIN

DISCOVERED IN 1739

Derived from the German word *kobold*, meaning goblin, cobalt was widely considered by fifteenth century miners as 'mischievous'. Not only did it play havoc with their health but it was often mistaken for silver, only to find it didn't smelt as expected. Later, its blue and green pigments were used for ceramics and it is particularly associated with China and Persia. It is also a key ingredient in the vitamin B_{12}, which helps your nervous system to function properly.

NICKEL

Ni

STATE AT 20°C
A silvery metal that resists corrosion.

WHERE ON EARTH?
Found in minerals such as pentlandite and garnierite.

DANGER TO LIFE
Essential to some species, but suspected to cause cancer and organ damage through repeated exposure.

SPECIAL USES
Toasters, electric ovens, armour plating, batteries.

ROCK ON

 DISCOVERED IN 1751

Aside from iron, nickel makes up much of the Earth's core. It is also found in meteorites, often alongside iron. That's no coincidence – planets like Earth were made when gravity pulled metallic space rocks together. You'll also find nickel in the strings of electric guitars, which were particularly popular with musicians in the 1960s. Famously it lends its name to the US five cent piece too, a tradition dating back to the 1800s when American coins were largely made of the 28th element.

ELECTRON CONFIGURATION

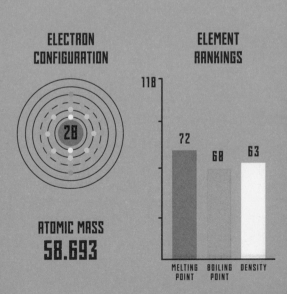

28

ATOMIC MASS
58.693

ELEMENT RANKINGS

118

72 — MELTING POINT
68 — BOILING POINT
63 — DENSITY

COPPER

STATE AT 20°C
A reddish-gold metal.

WHERE ON EARTH?
Found in minerals such as chalcopyrite and bornite.

DANGER TO LIFE
Essential to all living things: our bodies contain about 1.2 milligrams.

SPECIAL USES
Coins, electrical equipment, wires, motors.

WIRED UP

DISCOVERED IN ANCIENT TIMES

The first metal worked by humans, copper takes its name from the Latin *aes cuprum* or 'metal of Cyprus' as the country was an ancient source. That's where the element's Cu symbol comes from. The Bronze Age started when we discovered that mixing copper and tin together could form bronze – a good malleable conductor of heat that's more resistant to corrosion. Today, most copper is used in electrical equipment such as wiring and motors due to its ability to conduct heat and electricity.

ELECTRON CONFIGURATION

29

ATOMIC MASS
63.546

ELEMENT RANKINGS

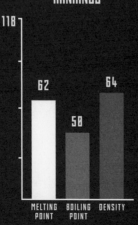

118

62
50
64

MELTING POINT | BOILING POINT | DENSITY

ZINC

STATE AT 20°C
A silvery-white metal with a blue tinge.

WHERE ON EARTH?
Found in several ores including zincblende and calamine.

DANGER TO LIFE
Essential to all living things; our bodies contain about 2.5 grams.

SPECIAL USES
Car bodies, street lamp posts, inks, soaps, batteries, textiles.

BRASSY TONES

 DISCOVERED IN 1746

Widely associated with music, zinc can be combined with copper to form the alloy brass, which helps create the bright, rich tones of brass instruments such as trumpets and horns. It is also commonly used to prevent rust by providing a thin coating to other metals – a process called galvanisation. A lack of zinc in food contributes to the deaths of 800,000 children a year worldwide, making it a very important part of a healthy diet.

ELECTRON CONFIGURATION

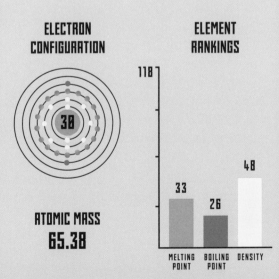

30

ATOMIC MASS
65.38

ELEMENT RANKINGS

118

33
MELTING POINT

26
BOILING POINT

48
DENSITY

GALLIUM

Ga

STATE AT 20°C
A soft, silvery-white metal.

WHERE ON EARTH?
Found in trace amounts in minerals such as bauxite and coal.

DANGER TO LIFE
No known biological role. It is non-toxic.

SPECIAL USES
Silicon substitute, LEDs, Blu-ray technology, solar panels.

HOT CHICKEN

 DISCOVERED IN 1875

Officially gallium was named after *Gallia*, an old Latin word for France because its discoverer, Paul Emile Lecoq, was French. But he may have sneakily named it after himself. Lecoq is the French word for 'rooster' which in Latin is *gallus*. A vital component of game consoles and Blu-ray players, gallium gives us high resolution, sharp colours and an awesome gaming experience. With a low melting point and high boiling point, gallium will readily melt in your hand.

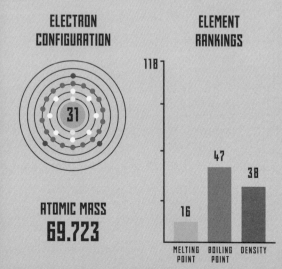

ELECTRON CONFIGURATION

31

ATOMIC MASS
69.723

ELEMENT RANKINGS

118

16
MELTING POINT

47
BOILING POINT

38
DENSITY

GERMANIUM

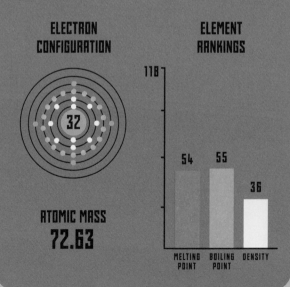

Ge

STATE AT 20°C
A grey-white semi-metal.

WHERE ON EARTH?
Found in the minerals germanite and argyrodite. it is very rare.

DANGER TO LIFE
No known biological role. It is non-toxic.

SPECIAL USES
Camera lenses, fluorescent lamps, microscopes.

OPTICAL AID

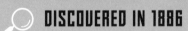 DISCOVERED IN 1886

Like its neighbour gallium, the shiny greyish-white germanium is also named after a country (Germany). The world's first transistor radio was made of this original semiconductor. These days it is combined with oxygen to make germania (GeO_2) which is a great material for use in optical devices, from the fibre-optic cables that carry internet and telephone signals, to the lenses in microscopes. Germanium was also used in the solar panels of two NASA Mars rovers.

ELECTRON CONFIGURATION

32

ATOMIC MASS
72.63

ELEMENT RANKINGS

118

54   55

36

MELTING POINT   BOILING POINT   DENSITY

ARSENIC

STATE AT 20°C
A silver-grey semi-metal.

WHERE ON EARTH?
Found mainly in the mineral arsenopyrite.

DANGER TO LIFE
Very toxic. Some foods contain arsenic in less harmful forms.

SPECIAL USES
Rat poisons, insecticides, poultry feed.

ELECTRON CONFIGURATION

33

ATOMIC MASS
74.922

ELEMENT RANKINGS

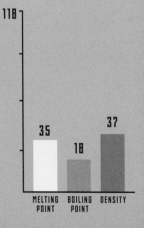

118

35 MELTING POINT
18 BOILING POINT
37 DENSITY

DEATHLY POISON

 DISCOVERED IN APPROX. 1250

Famed for its incredibly toxic properties, this poisonous element has been associated with many famous deaths throughout history and is sometimes called 'the poison of kings'. The British king, George III famously went mad, possibly because his wigs contained high levels of arsenic. Robert Bunsen invented a cure for arsenic poisoning and then needed it years later after an explosion in his laboratory. We get the element's name from the Syrian *al zarniqa* which means yellow- or gold-coloured.

SELENIUM

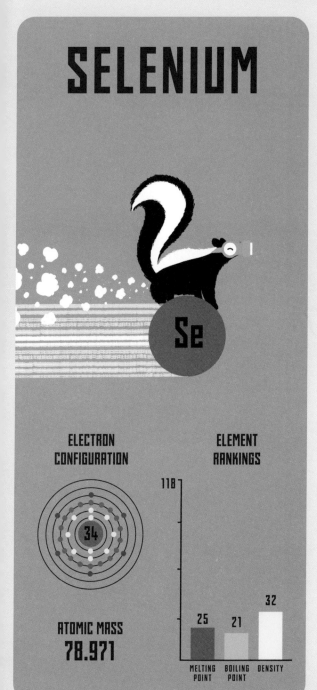

Se

ELECTRON CONFIGURATION

34

ATOMIC MASS
78.971

ELEMENT RANKINGS

118

MELTING POINT	BOILING POINT	DENSITY
25	21	32

STATE AT 20°C
A silvery semi-metal or red powder.

WHERE ON EARTH?
Found in a few rare minerals.

DANGER TO LIFE
Essential to humans (our bodies contain about 14mg) but toxic if ingested in high doses.

SPECIAL USES
Paint, plastics, photocopiers, night vision cameras.

STINKY SKUNK

 DISCOVERED IN 1817

Named after a moon goddess due to its similar properties to tellurium (which was named after the Roman goddess of Earth), selenium is the ingredient that makes a skunk's spray so potent. You're more likely to encounter it in glasses and ceramics where it is used to lend a red colour. Like its neighbour, arsenic, it is poisonous in large quantities, but small amounts of it are crucial for humans. It helps your thyroid function properly – a gland in your neck that produces important hormones.

BROMINE

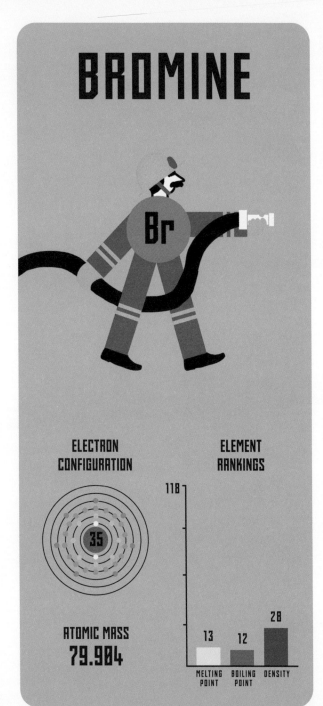

Br

ELECTRON CONFIGURATION

35

ATOMIC MASS
79.904

ELEMENT RANKINGS

118

MELTING POINT	BOILING POINT	DENSITY
13	12	28

STATE AT 20°C
A deep red, oily liquid with a strong smell.

WHERE ON EARTH?
Found in seawater and brine deposits.

DANGER TO LIFE
No known biological role in humans, but highly dangerous if bromine vapour is inhaled.

SPECIAL USES
Agricultural chemicals, insecticides, film photography.

FIRE FIGHTER
 ## DISCOVERED IN 1826

Another element famed for its unpleasant smell, bromine is named after the Greek word for 'stench'. This element is rare in the Earth's crust, but more common in seawater which is the main source of the bromine used in agriculture and pharmaceuticals. Bromine compounds are excellent flame retardants but usage in fire extinguishers was banned in 1994 as bromine atoms destroy the ozone layer. Despite this, they are still commonly used to make firefighter uniforms.

KRYPTON

Kr

STATE AT 20°C
A colourless, unreactive gas with no smell.

WHERE ON EARTH?
Found in the Earth's atmosphere. It is one of the rarest gases.

DANGER TO LIFE
No known biological role. It is non-toxic.

SPECIAL USES
Energy-saving fluorescent lights, photography, lasers.

ELECTRON CONFIGURATION

36

ATOMIC MASS
83.798

ELEMENT RANKINGS

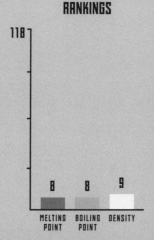

118

MELTING POINT	BOILING POINT	DENSITY
8	8	9

SUPER-RARE

DISCOVERED IN 1898

Krypton's name is derived from the Greek word for 'hidden' because it was so hard to find – it is still one of the rarest gases on Earth. The little krypton we do have is useful in photography and lighting. It shares a similar name to the fictional material kryptonite – Superman's Achilles heel – but his enemy Lex Luthor reveals that it is made of 'sodium lithium boron silicate hydroxide with fluorine', so no krypton. Instead it is named after Superman's home planet.

RUBIDIUM

STATE AT 20°C
A soft metal that reacts violently with water and ignites in the air.

WHERE ON EARTH?
Found in the minerals pollucite, carnallite, leucite and lepidolite.

DANGER TO LIFE
No known biological role. It is non-toxic, but dangerous if ingested as it reacts with water.

SPECIAL USES
The purple colour in fireworks, scientific research.

THE DETECTOR
 DISCOVERED IN 1861

Rubidium is named after its vibrant, rich colour from the Latin word *rubidus*, meaning 'dark red'. Reacting violently with water, igniting with air and melting easily, rubidium is normally stored in kerosene. It has little use outside of scientific research, but has proven to be an excellent detector of cancerous cells in the body and a key component of super-accurate timekeepers called atomic clocks. It is also the first alkali metal to have a density higher than water, meaning it sinks.

ELECTRON CONFIGURATION
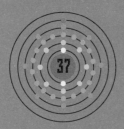
37

ATOMIC MASS
85.468

ELEMENT RANKINGS
118

MELTING POINT	BOILING POINT	DENSITY
17	22	15

STRONTIUM

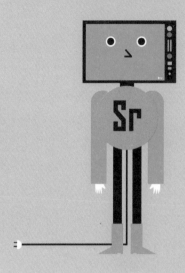

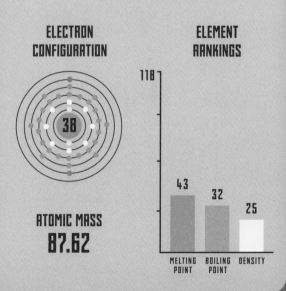

STATE AT 28°C
A soft, silvery metal that reacts with water and ignites in the air.

WHERE ON EARTH?
Found in the minerals celestite and strontianite.

DANGER TO LIFE
No known biological role in humans. It is non-toxic.

SPECIAL USES
The red colour in fireworks, glow-in-the-dark paints.

PIXEL PERFECT

 ## DISCOVERED IN 1790

Named after Strontian, the Scottish village where it was discovered, strontium's primary use is in television sets, although this is changing as we switch towards more sophisticated, modern screens. Like its upstairs neighbour calcium, it's easily absorbed into bones and used for bone tumour treatments. Strontium-90, its radioactive isotope, can be used to generate electricity for space vehicles. You'll also find strontium in toothpaste for people with sensitive teeth.

ELECTRON CONFIGURATION

38

ATOMIC MASS
87.62

ELEMENT RANKINGS

118

43
MELTING POINT

32
BOILING POINT

25
DENSITY

38

YTTRIUM

STATE AT 20°C
A soft, silvery metal.

WHERE ON EARTH?
Found in minerals such as xenotime, monazite and bastnaesite.

DANGER TO LIFE
No known biological role. It is mildly toxic.

SPECIAL USES
Microwave filters, camera lenses, lasers, medical use.

OXYGEN THIEF

 DISCOVERED IN 1794

The name yttrium originates from a Swedish village called Ytterby where the element was discovered alongside several others. It is a fantastic super-conductor, and can also increase the strength of aluminium and magnesium alloys. It is also known as the 'oxygen thief' due to its ability to dissolve oxygen. You'll find it inside Light Emitting Diodes or LEDs, an increasingly popular form of lighting. It's toxic in high quantities and can cause lung disease.

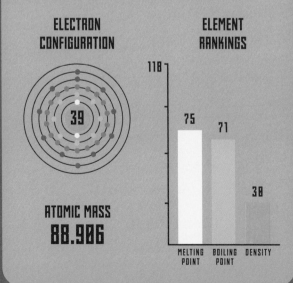

ELECTRON CONFIGURATION

39

ATOMIC MASS
88.906

ELEMENT RANKINGS

118

75
71
30

MELTING POINT | BOILING POINT | DENSITY

ZIRCONIUM

Zr

ELECTRON CONFIGURATION

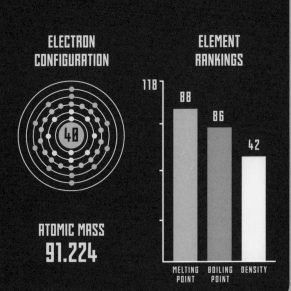

48

ATOMIC MASS
91.224

ELEMENT RANKINGS

118

88

86

42

MELTING POINT

BOILING POINT

DENSITY

STATE AT 20°C
A hard, grey-white metal that resists corrosion.

WHERE ON EARTH?
Found in about 30 different minerals, including zircon.

DANGER TO LIFE
No known biological role. It is mildly toxic.

SPECIAL USES
Nuclear power stations, ceramics, cosmetics, microwave filters.

DR DURABLE

 DISCOVERED IN 1789

This greyish-white metal is commonly used in surgeon's tools and dentistry due to its durability and resistance to heat and corrosion by acids, alkalis and salt water. The same properties make it invaluable for space rockets, aircraft and nuclear power stations. It is often produced as a by-product of tin mining. Precious stones containing zirconium have been known since ancient times and it offers a cheaper alternative to diamonds. When turned into a powder it becomes highly flammable.

NIOBIUM

Nb

ELECTRON CONFIGURATION

41

ATOMIC MASS
92.906

ELEMENT RANKINGS

118

97 — MELTING POINT
98 — BOILING POINT
59 — DENSITY

STATE AT 20°C
A silvery metal that resists corrosion.

WHERE ON EARTH?
Found in the mineral columbite.

DANGER TO LIFE
No known biological role. It is mildly toxic.

SPECIAL USES
Stainless steel, jet engines, rockets, optical glasses.

BLUE TEARS
DISCOVERED IN 1801

Named after the Greek goddess of tears, Niobe, niobium changes its silvery hue to blue, green or yellow when exposed to the air and has a high resistance to corrosion and heat. It is often found in nature together with the element tantalum, and is therefore known as the 'daughter' of the mythical Greek king Tantalus. It is quite hard to tell the difference between the two. Niobium has a wide range of uses, from jewellery to the MRI scanners you'll find in hospitals.

MOLYBDENUM

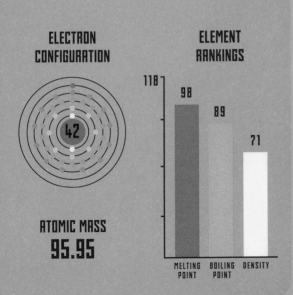

Mo

STATE AT 20°C
A shiny, silvery metal.

WHERE ON EARTH?
Found in the ore molybdenite.

DANGER TO LIFE
Essential for animals and plants. It is toxic in high doses.

SPECIAL USES
Steel knives, engines, saws, drills, circuit boards, rockets.

STEEL CUTLERY
DISCOVERED IN 1781

Found in enzymes in your intestine, it would be impossible to digest food without molybdenum in our bodies. Good sources of molybdenum include green beans, eggs and cucumbers. However, it is toxic in high doses. It is used in steel alloys to increase strength which makes excellent knives. It takes its name from molybdenite, from the Greek word *molybdos*, meaning 'lead' because molybdenite and lead ore were often accidentally mistaken for one another.

ELECTRON CONFIGURATION

42

ATOMIC MASS
95.95

ELEMENT RANKINGS

118

98

89

71

MELTING POINT

BOILING POINT

DENSITY

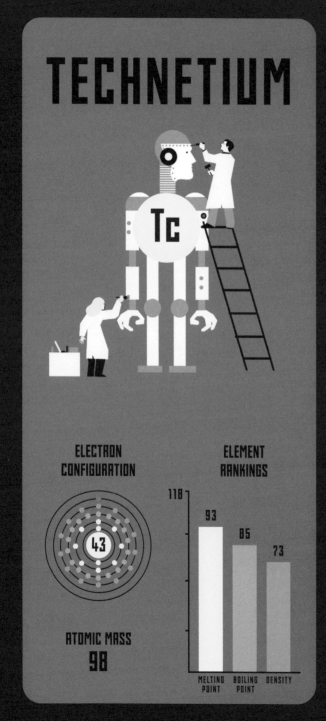

TECHNETIUM

Tc

ELECTRON CONFIGURATION

(43)

ATOMIC MASS
98

ELEMENT RANKINGS

118

93 | 85 | 73

MELTING POINT | BOILING POINT | DENSITY

STATE AT 20°C
A silvery metal.

WHERE ON EARTH?
Produced from the fission products of uranium nuclear fuel.

DANGER TO LIFE
No known biological role. It is radioactive and toxic.

SPECIAL USES
Medical diagnosis, radioactive tracer for imaging scans.

HUMAN ROBOT

 **DISCOVERED IN 1937**

Technetium was the first element to be manufactured by humans, rather than found naturally, hence the name is based on the word 'technology'. However, technetium was also later discovered in red giants – stars that are nearing the ends of their lives. Technetium is the lightest element that is radioactive in all its forms. That makes it unstable and short-lived, but it still has important uses in medical diagnosis. It was one of the 'missing' elements predicted by Mendeleev.

RUTHENIUM

Ru

STATE AT 20°C
A hard, shiny, silvery metal.

WHERE ON EARTH?
Found in minerals such as pentlandite and pyroxenite.

DANGER TO LIFE
No known biological role. Some compounds are highly toxic.

SPECIAL USES
Electronics industry, solar cells, hard drives, fountain pens.

ELECTRON CONFIGURATION

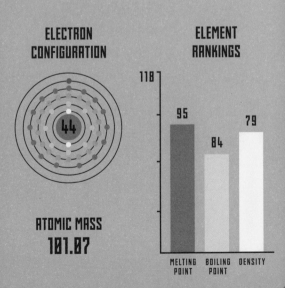

44

ATOMIC MASS
101.07

ELEMENT RANKINGS

118

95

84

79

MELTING POINT | BOILING POINT | DENSITY

HARD KICKS

 DISCOVERED IN 1844

Sourced from the Ural mountains in Russia, ruthenium takes its name from the Latin word for that country (*Ruthenia*). It is one of the rarest metals on Earth. Hardy and resistant to tarnishing, ruthenium is often alloyed with platinum to create wear-resistant electronics and jewellery. Fountain pen tips are often made of ruthenium. Due to the ability of some ruthenium compounds to absorb sunlight, scientists are experimenting to see if it could be used in the solar panels of the future.

RHODIUM

Rh

ELECTRON CONFIGURATION

45

ATOMIC MASS
102.906

ELEMENT RANKINGS

110

91

77

88

MELTING POINT | BOILING POINT | DENSITY

STATE AT 20°C
A hard, silvery-white metal.

WHERE ON EARTH?
Found in river sands and copper-nickel sulfide ores.

DANGER TO LIFE
No known biological role; compound are considered highly toxic.

SPECIAL USES
Catalytic converters for cars, optic fibres, optical mirrors.

RARE ROSE

DISCOVERED IN 1803

Named after the Greek word for 'rose' due to its pink hue, rhodium is a silvery-white and hard metal. It is one of the rarest elements, making it relatively expensive. It is often used today in catalytic converters that reduce the amount of polluting gases in cars, vans and motorbikes. You'll also find it used to make fibreglass – a strong and lightweight plastic material for engineering and construction – and in the manufacturing of mirrors.

PALLADIUM

Pd

ATOMIC MASS
106.42

ELEMENT RANKINGS

118

81

62

78

MELTING POINT | BOILING POINT | DENSITY

STATE AT 20°C
A shiny, silvery-white metal that resists corrosion.

WHERE ON EARTH?
Found mainly in sulfide minerals such as braggite.

DANGER TO LIFE
No known biological role. It is non-toxic.

SPECIAL USES
Hydrogen fuel cells, mobile phones, dental fillings.

BALLS OF FIRE

 DISCOVERED IN 1803

Palladium gets its name from Pallas, one of the largest asteroids in the asteroid belt between the orbits of Mars and Jupiter. The asteroid itself was named after the ancient Greek goddess Pallas Athena. Palladium has a wide range of uses, from catalytic converters to jewellery and dentistry. It is also found in laptops and mobile phones, where it is used to plate electrical connections. At one point palladium chloride was used to treat tuberculosis, although more effective methods are now used.

SILVER

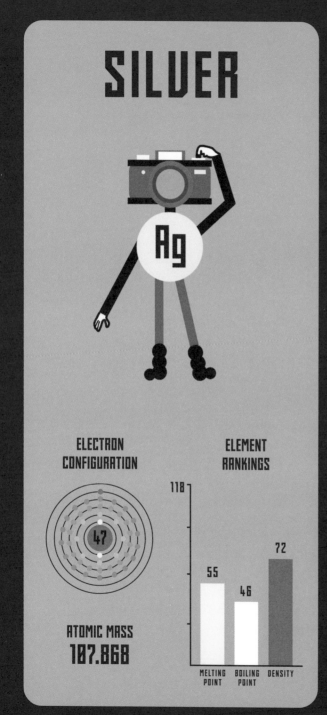

Ag

ELECTRON CONFIGURATION

47

ATOMIC MASS
107.868

ELEMENT RANKINGS

118

MELTING POINT	BOILING POINT	DENSITY
55	46	72

STATE AT 20°C
A soft, shiny metal that tarnishes slowly in air.

WHERE ON EARTH?
Found uncombined in nature and in ores such as argentite.

DANGER TO LIFE
No known biological role. It is non-toxic.

SPECIAL USES
Jewellery, silver tableware, mirrors, batteries, gloves.

SAY CHEESE!

 ## DISCOVERED IN ANCIENT TIMES

One of the first precious metals discovered by humans, we've used silver for over 7,000 years. There's even a country named after it – Argentina comes from *argentum*, Latin for 'silver' and the origin of its Ag chemical symbol. Silver is valued in jewellery because it has the highest reflectivity of any metal. It's also the best metallic electrical conductor so is widely used in electrical appliances, including cameras. Its antibacterial properties see it used in wound dressings, too.

CADMIUM

STATE AT 20°C
A silvery-white metal with a bluish tinge on its surface.

WHERE ON EARTH?
Found in the mineral greenockite.

DANGER TO LIFE
Toxic and carcinogenic. It is also in our bodies: about 50 milligrams.

SPECIAL USES
Limited use due to its toxicity.

YELLOW PAINT
DISCOVERED IN 1817

This silvery-white element – similar to zinc and mercury – gives its name to cadmium pigments in paint including yellow, orange and red. Coincidentally is also the name of a famous art piece painted by Jean-Michel Basquiat, which is made from cadmium paints. Its high toxicity to humans means its usage is limited. Most of our cadmium supplies come from Asia, with China, South Korea and Japan among the top producers. It ends up in rechargeable batteries, television sets and the reactors found in nuclear power plants.

ELECTRON CONFIGURATION

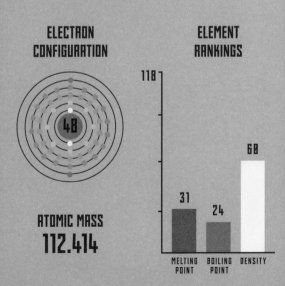

48

ATOMIC MASS
112.414

ELEMENT RANKINGS

118

60
31
24

MELTING POINT | BOILING POINT | DENSITY

INDIUM

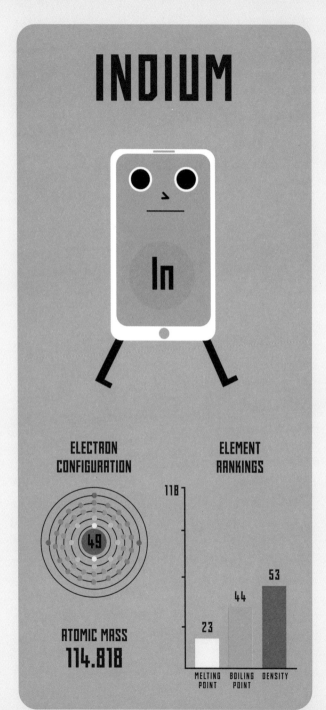

In

ELECTRON CONFIGURATION

49

ATOMIC MASS
114.818

ELEMENT RANKINGS

118

MELTING POINT	BOILING POINT	DENSITY
23	44	53

STATE AT 20°C
A soft, silvery metal.

WHERE ON EARTH?
Found in zinc minerals and iron, lead and copper ores.

DANGER TO LIFE
No known biological role. It is toxic.

SPECIAL USES
Fire-sprinkler systems, mirror finish for windows, microchips.

TOUCHSCREEN

 DISCOVERED IN 1863

Important for touchscreen technology and liquid crystal displays (LCDs), modern day smartphones and tablets would not be possible without indium. Indium tin oxide is transparent, conduct electricity and bonds strongly to glass. Its name is derived from the vibrant indigo light it shows in a spectroscope. One of its first uses was in the engines of aircraft deployed during World War II. Many modern thermometers no longer use mercury, replacing it with a gallium-indium-tin alloy instead.

TIN

Sn

ELECTRON CONFIGURATION

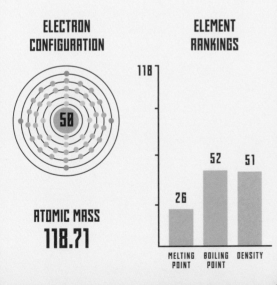

50

ATOMIC MASS
118.71

ELEMENT RANKINGS

	118		
	26	52	51
	MELTING POINT	BOILING POINT	DENSITY

STATE AT 20°C
A soft, malleable metal.

WHERE ON EARTH?
Mainly found in the ore cassiterite.

DANGER TO LIFE
No known biological role in humans. It has low toxicity.

SPECIAL USES
Tin cans, window glass, toys, solder, ceramics, plastics.

ORGAN GRINDER

 DISCOVERED IN ANCIENT TIMES

Known since antiquity, tin is a soft, malleable metal that alloys to form bronze. It is commonly found in Thailand, China and Indonesia – an area referred to as the 'tin belt'. It has a variety of uses, one of which includes making the pipes for church organs. Tin is also widely used in soldering – the act of joining electrical components with molten metal. In folklore, tin whistles are commonly associated with witches. Its Sn symbol comes from its Latin name, *stannum*.

ANTIMONY

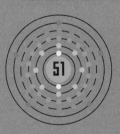

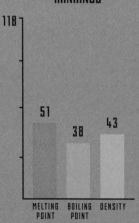

ELECTRON CONFIGURATION

51

ATOMIC MASS
121.76

ELEMENT RANKINGS

118

MELTING POINT	BOILING POINT	DENSITY
51	38	43

STATE AT 20°C
A hard, silvery and brittle semi-metal.

WHERE ON EARTH?
Found in small quantities in over 100 minerals.

DANGER TO LIFE
Toxic. It can cause liver damage in large doses.

SPECIAL USES
Infrared detectors, batteries, bullets, paints, glass.

CLEO'S EYE

 DISCOVERED IN ANCIENT TIMES

Dating back to ancient Egypt, this element was used to create a rich, black kohl for eyeliner. Antimony also produces a bright yellow pigment popular in glassware and paint. This yellow hue is often referred to as 'Naples Yellow', as natural deposits of the substance were thought to be abundant around Mount Vesuvius, nea the Italian city. Today, antimony is an effective flame retardant and is also used in infrared devices.

TELLURIUM

Te

STATE AT 20°C
A metalloid: usually
a grey powder.

WHERE ON EARTH?
Found in the minerals tellurite,
calaverite and sylvanite.

DANGER TO LIFE
No known biological role.
It is very toxic.

SPECIAL USES
Alloys, solar cells, CDs, DVDs,
mini-fridges, rubber.

ELECTRON CONFIGURATION

52

ATOMIC MASS
127.6

ELEMENT RANKINGS

118

MELTING POINT	BOILING POINT	DENSITY
34	28	41

GARLIC BREATH

 DISCOVERED IN 1783

Tellurium is named after the Latin
word *tellus* meaning 'Earth'.
Ironically, it is one of the rarest
elements on our planet, but is
abundant in space. It is toxic and can
be very dangerous to your health.
If you breathe in as little as
0.01 mg/m^3, you'll release a foul
garlic-like odour known as 'tellurium
breath'. When added to steel and
copper, it produces alloys that are
easier for a machine to process.

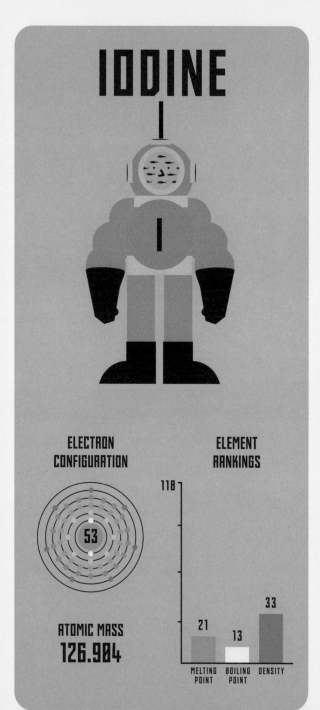

IODINE

ELECTRON CONFIGURATION

53

ATOMIC MASS
126.904

ELEMENT RANKINGS

118

21	13	33
MELTING POINT	BOILING POINT	DENSITY

STATE AT 20°C
A black shiny solid or purple vapour.

WHERE ON EARTH?
Found in seawater; iodide and iodate minerals.

DANGER TO LIFE
Essential for humans (our bodies contain up to 20mg) but toxic if ingested.

SPECIAL USES
Animal feed, LCD displays. printing inks, dyes.

UNDERWATER

 DISCOVERED IN 1811

This element was first discovered among seaweed that had been dried and burned. It is the heaviest stable halogen and the heaviest essential nutrient in the human diet. An iodine deficiency can stop your thyroid gland from working properly. Fish, dairy products and eggs are all good sources of iodine. Today, iodine is found in disinfectants, pharmaceuticals and photographic chemicals. It is also used in the controversial method of 'cloud seeding' to induce rainfall.

XENON

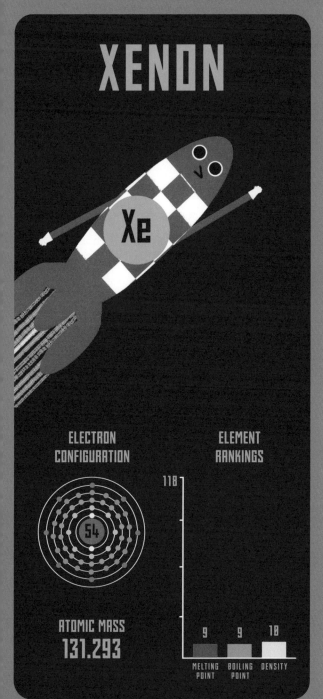

Xe

ELECTRON CONFIGURATION

54

ATOMIC MASS
131.293

ELEMENT RANKINGS

118

MELTING POINT	BOILING POINT	DENSITY
9	9	18

STATE AT 20°C

An unreactive, colourless, odourless gas.

WHERE ON EARTH?

Found in the atmosphere and in the gases from some mineral springs.

DANGER TO LIFE

No known biological role. Non-toxic but its compounds are highly toxic.

SPECIAL USES

Plasma displays, general anaesthetic, sunbed lamps,

ROCKET FUEL

 DISCOVERED IN 1898

This rare element was one of the last noble gases to be isolated. Xenon produces an extremely bright, bluish-white light when an electrical current is passed through it, useful in photographic flashes and lighting equipment. It is also a component for ion engines in spacecraft. It allows them to travel incredibly quickly in space using only a small amount of fuel. Xenon engines are about 10 times as powerful as rocket engines!

CAESIUM

Cs

STATE AT 20°C
A soft, gold coloured metal.

WHERE ON EARTH?
Found in the minerals pollucite and lepidolite.

DANGER TO LIFE
No known biological role. Toxic if ingested as reacts violently with water.

SPECIAL USES
Drilling fluid, optical glass, vacuum tubes.

ELECTRON CONFIGURATION

55

ATOMIC MASS
132.905

ELEMENT RANKINGS

110

15 — MELTING POINT
20 — BOILING POINT
20 — DENSITY

NEVER LATE

DISCOVERED IN 1860

Caesium is named after the Latin word *caesius*, meaning 'sky blue' and refers to the bright blue lines in its spectrum. Uniquely, it is used to define the length of a second. The caesium-133 atom switches between two electron configurations 9,192,631,770 a second. Clocks that use caesium are so accurate that they can tick for one hundred million years without losing a second of time.

BARIUM

STATE AT 20°C
A soft, silvery-white metal that reacts quickly.

WHERE ON EARTH?
Found in the ores barite and witherite.

DANGER TO LIFE
No known biological role. It is toxic.

SPECIAL USES
Paint, glassmaking, rat poison, green colour in fireworks.

X-RAY VISION

DISCOVERED IN 1808

This soft, silvery metal tarnishes easily and reacts with water. It is also toxic in high quantities. Barium can be swallowed by medical patients to help doctors check their stomach and intestines on X-rays, as it helps to show abnormalities more clearly. It was first used in this way as far back as 1908. Barium is also alloyed with nickel to make the spark plugs in car engines and barium titanium silicate is a very rare gemstone that is the official gem of California, USA.

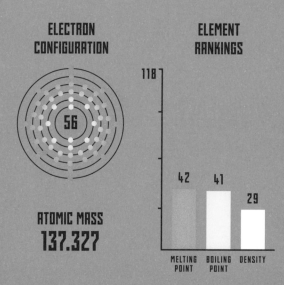

ELECTRON CONFIGURATION

56

ATOMIC MASS
137.327

ELEMENT RANKINGS

118

42	41	29
MELTING POINT	BOILING POINT	DENSITY

LANTHANUM

La

ELECTRON CONFIGURATION

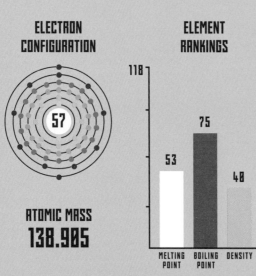

57

ATOMIC MASS
138.905

ELEMENT RANKINGS

118

53

75

40

MELTING POINT | BOILING POINT | DENSITY

STATE AT 20°C
A soft, silvery-white metal that reacts quickly.

WHERE ON EARTH?
Found in minerals such as bastnaesite and monazite.

DANGER TO LIFE
No known biological role. It is moderately toxic and reacts violently with water.

SPECIAL USES
Hybrid cars, lighter flints, optical glasses.

AT THE MOVIES

DISCOVERED IN 1839

The first member of the lanthanides, lanthanum's name is derived from the Greek word *lanthano* meaning 'to lie hidden'. Lanthanum is extensively used in carbon lights, particularly cinema projectors. We also put it into the nickel-metal hydride batteries used in hybrid cars – vehicles that run partly on electricity and partly on traditional fuel. Small amounts are added to outdoor swimming pools to remove the phosphates that algae feed on, and so stop the water from turning green.

CERIUM

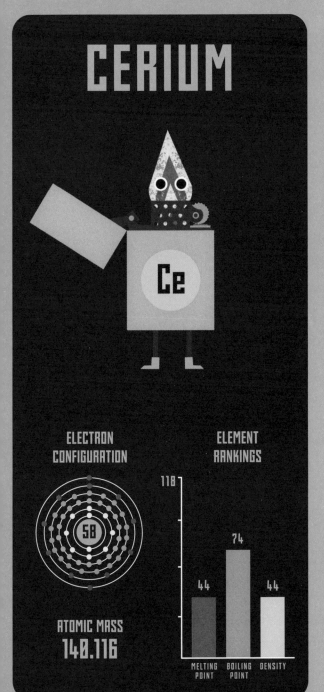

Ce

ELECTRON CONFIGURATION

58

ELEMENT RANKINGS

118

44
74
44

MELTING POINT
BOILING POINT
DENSITY

ATOMIC MASS
140.116

STATE AT 20°C
A grey, reactive metal.

WHERE ON EARTH?
Found in minerals such as bastnaesite and monazite.

DANGER TO LIFE
No known biological role. It is moderately toxic.

SPECIAL USES
Self-cleaning ovens, sunglasses, flat-screen TVs.

LIGHT MY FIRE

DISCOVERED IN 1803

Named after the dwarf planet and largest asteroid, Ceres, cerium is soft enough to be cut with a knife. It is the most abundant of all the lanthanides and tarnishes in air, forming a layer on the outside not dissimilar to rust. Cerium makes sparks and burns when heated, making it ideal for use in lighters. It makes fire, but it can also fight its effects. The compound cerium nitrate is used to prevent patients with serious burns from getting infections.

PRASEODYMIUM

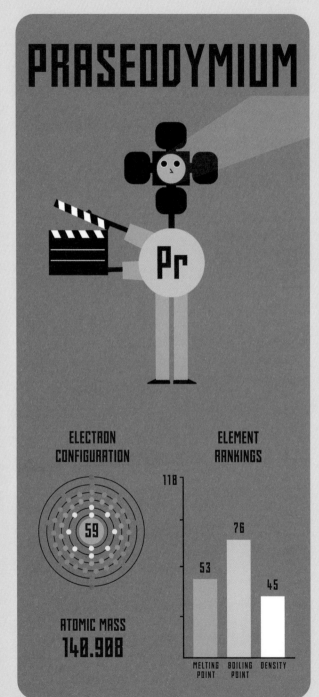

Pr

STATE AT 20°C
A soft, silvery metal.

WHERE ON EARTH?
Found in minerals such as monazite and bastnaesite.

DANGER TO LIFE
No known biological role. Known to catch fire spontaneously on exposure to air.

SPECIAL USES
Aircraft engines. magnets. studio lighting, goggles.

IT'S A WRAP

 DISCOVERED IN 1885

Praseodymium was discovered at the same time as neodymium, its neighbour in the periodic table. Its name reflects this, coming from the Greek words *prasinos*, meaning 'green' and *didymos*, meaning 'twin'. Praseodymium is used to give glasses, enamels and ceramics a yellow colour. It is also a key ingredient in the carbon arc lamps used by film studios to light scenes when shooting a movie. Alloyed with magnesium, it makes a strong metal used in plane engines.

ELECTRON CONFIGURATION

59

ATOMIC MASS
140.908

ELEMENT RANKINGS

118

76

53

45

MELTING POINT	BOILING POINT	DENSITY

NEODYMIUM

STATE AT 20°C
A silvery-white metal that tarnishes quickly in air.

WHERE ON EARTH?
Found in minerals such as monazite and bastnaesite.

DANGER TO LIFE
No known biological role. It is moderately toxic.

SPECIAL USES
Car windscreen wipers, tanning booths, wind turbines.

SUPER MAGNET

 DISCOVERED IN 1885

When used as an alloy with iron and boron, neodymium magnets are the strongest in the world. They're often referred to as super magnets and can lift up to 1,000 times their own weight. Neodymium appears wherever small magnets are needed, whether that be in microphones, loudspeakers, headphones or inside computers. It is also used in some lasers for magnetic purposes. Adding neodymium oxide (Nd_2O_3) to molten glass gives it a variety of bright colours when it cools.

ELECTRON CONFIGURATION

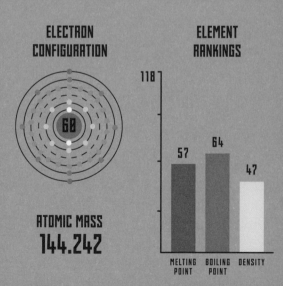

60

ATOMIC MASS
144.242

ELEMENT RANKINGS

118

MELTING POINT	BOILING POINT	DENSITY
57	64	47

PROMETHIUM

Pm

STATE AT 20°C
A radioactive metal.

WHERE ON EARTH?
Manufactured, not found naturally on Earth.

DANGER TO LIFE
No known biological role. It is highly toxic.

SPECIAL USES
Mainly used in research, atomic batteries, X-rays.

LUMINOUS FIRE

 DISCOVERED IN 1945

This element is named after the Titan Prometheus, who in Greek mythology stole fire from the gods to give to humankind. Promethium was one of the last lanthanides to be discovered and is normally only created inside a laboratory. It does occur naturally in the Earth's crust, but in such vanishingly small amounts that there is only ever 500 grams in existence at any one time. As such it has little use outside of research, although it is found in some luminous paints.

ELECTRON CONFIGURATION

61

ATOMIC MASS
145

ELEMENT RANKINGS

118

MELTING POINT — 58
BOILING POINT — 63
DENSITY — 58

SAMARIUM

STATE AT 20°C
A silvery-white metal.

WHERE ON EARTH?
Found in minerals such as monazite and bastnaesite.

DANGER TO LIFE
No known biological role. It has low toxicity.

SPECIAL USES
Headphones, personal stereos, optical lasers, glass, ceramics.

SOLAR FLIGHT

 DISCOVERED IN 1879

Named for the mineral samarskite, which was discovered by a Russian miner called Colonel Vasili Samarsky-Bykhovets, samarium became the first element to be named after a person. Later it was used to make the motors of *Solar Challenger*, the first solar-powered plane capable of long-distance flights. More often you'll find it in the samarium-cobalt magnets used in electric guitars. Like other lanthanides, it is also used in studio lighting and projection.

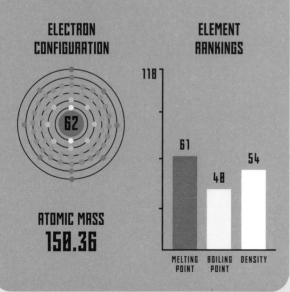

ELECTRON CONFIGURATION

62

ATOMIC MASS
150.36

ELEMENT RANKINGS

118

61

48

54

MELTING POINT | BOILING POINT | DENSITY

EUROPIUM

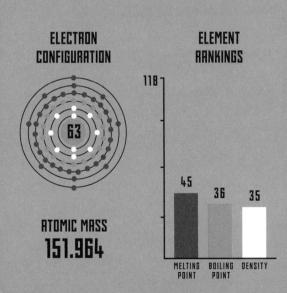

STATE AT 20°C
A soft, silvery metal that tarnishes quickly in air.

WHERE ON EARTH?
Found in minerals such as monazite and bastnaesite.

DANGER TO LIFE
No known biological role. It has low toxicity, but reacts violentl with water, so should not be ingested

SPECIAL USES
Watches, alarm clocks, luminous paint, low-energy light bulbs.

EURO-CASH

 DISCOVERED IN 1981

Originally identified from an impurity discovered in samarium-gadolinium concentrates, europium has since been discovered on the Moon, in the Sun and some other stars. It is the most reactive of the lanthanides, quickly oxidising in air and reacting vigorously with water. Interestingly, not only is the element named for Europe, but it is coincidentally also used in printing euro banknotes to prevent counterfeiting. It is one of the rarest of the rare Earth metals.

ELECTRON CONFIGURATION

63

ATOMIC MASS
151.964

ELEMENT RANKINGS

118

MELTING POINT	BOILING POINT	DENSITY
45	36	35

GADOLINIUM

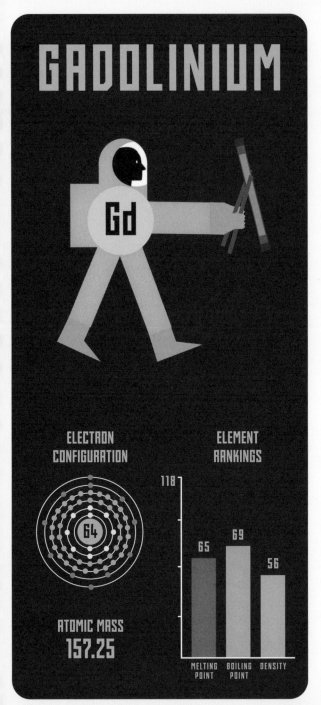

Gd

ELECTRON CONFIGURATION

64

ELEMENT RANKINGS

118

65 69 56

MELTING POINT | BOILING POINT | DENSITY

ATOMIC MASS
157.25

STATE AT 20°C
A silvery-white metal that reacts with oxygen and water.

WHERE ON EARTH?
Found in minerals such as monazite and bastnaesite.

DANGER TO LIFE
No known biological role. It has low toxicity.

SPECIAL USES
Nuclear reactors, magnets, data storage disks.

NUCLEAR CORE

 DISCOVERED IN 1880

Gadolinium is obtained from gadolinite, a mineral named for the Finnish chemist Johan Gadolin. It's a silvery-white metal that tarnishes easily when exposed to the air. Gadolinium has a wide range of uses, from making magnets and electronic components to the core of nuclear reactors. Perhaps its most important contribution to our lives is in medical devices. It's used to target tumours in one form of cancer treatment and helps take the images in X-ray and MRI machines.

TERBIUM

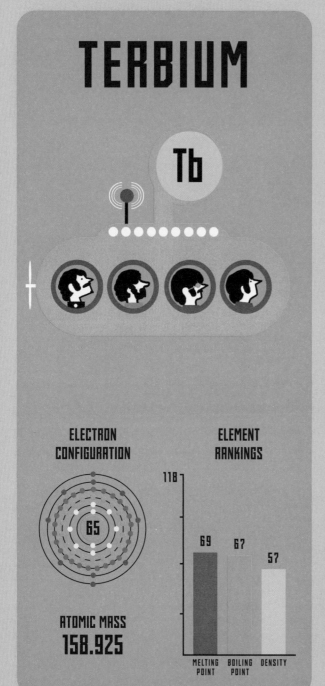

Tb

ELECTRON CONFIGURATION

65

ATOMIC MASS
158.925

ELEMENT RANKINGS

118

69 67

57

MELTING POINT | BOILING POINT | DENSITY

STATE AT 20°C
A soft, silvery metal.

WHERE ON EARTH?
Found in minerals such as monazite and bastnaesite.

DANGER TO LIFE
No known biological role. It has low toxicity.

SPECIAL USES
Low-energy light bulbs, mercury lamps, laser devices.

Y-SUBMARINE
 DISCOVERED IN 1843

The second element to be discovered in the Swedish town of Ytterby, inside a gadolinite ore, terbium is a versatile element which is malleable, ductile and reacts slowly with cold water. The control rods of nuclear submarines are made of terbium and it is also used in naval sonar systems. Terbium salts are sometimes used in lasers and as an anti-counterfeiting measure in bank notes. It's also used in electric bicycles and magnetic glass.

DYSPROSIUM

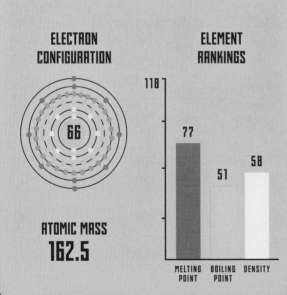

STATE AT 20°C

A bright, silvery metal that reacts quickly.

WHERE ON EARTH?

Found in minerals such as monazite and bastnaesite.

DANGER TO LIFE

No known biological role. It has low toxicity.

SPECIAL USES

Wind turbines, electrical vehicles, nuclear reactor control rods.

CLEAN ENERGY

 DISCOVERED IN 1886

It took until the 1950s to fully isolate this silvery, metallic element. So it is appropriate that its name originates from the Greek word *dysprositos* meaning 'hard to get at'. Dysprosium is often used for hybrid motors, wind turbine engines and computer storage, meaning there has been an increase in demand for it in recent years. According to the United States Department of Energy, dysprosium is the single most critical element for emerging clean energy technologies.

ELECTRON CONFIGURATION

66

ATOMIC MASS
162.5

ELEMENT RANKINGS

118

77

51

58

MELTING POINT | BOILING POINT | DENSITY

HOLMIUM

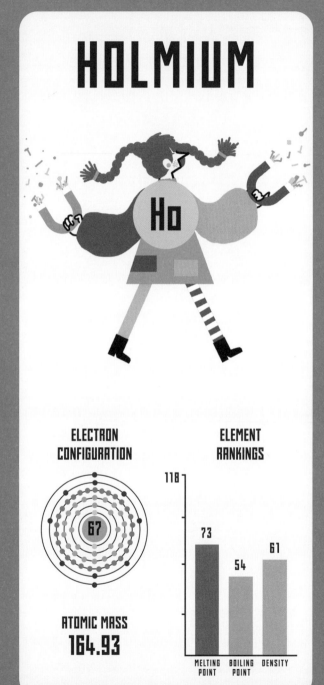

Ho

ELECTRON CONFIGURATION

67

ATOMIC MASS
164.93

ELEMENT RANKINGS

118

73

54

61

MELTING POINT | BOILING POINT | DENSITY

STATE AT 20°C
A bright, silvery metal.

WHERE ON EARTH?
Found in minerals such as monazite and bastnaesite.

DANGER TO LIFE
No known biological role. It is non-toxic.

SPECIAL USES
Nuclear reactors, magnets, lasers.

MAGNET POWER

 DISCOVERED IN 1878

The name comes from *Holmia*, the Latin word for the city of Stockholm. Holmium has the highest magnetic strength of any element, along with some other very unusual magnetic properties, and researchers are still trying to work out how we can utilise that to our advantage. So far we've used it in nuclear reactors, lasers and as another way to colour glass. It may be possible to use it in quantum computers in the future.

ERBIUM

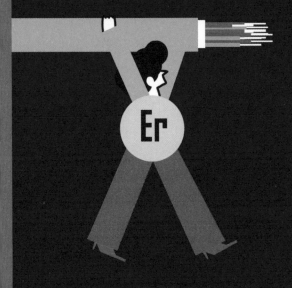

STATE AT 20°C
A soft, silvery metal.

WHERE ON EARTH?
Found in minerals such as monazite and bastnaesite.

DANGER TO LIFE
No known biological role. It has low toxicity.

SPECIAL USES
Safety glasses, sunglasses, fake gems, broadband signals.

FIBRE OPTIC

 DISCOVERED IN 1843

Erbium is commonly used today in fibre optic cables, where it helps to amplify the broadband and telephone signals they deliver to our homes. We inadvertently consume about one milligram of erbium a year, but it is not toxic to us in such small quantities. An erbium-nickel alloy is used in cryocoolers – small table-top refrigeration units that can bring their contents down to temperatures around minus 180 degrees Celsius.

ELECTRON CONFIGURATION

68

ELEMENT RANKINGS

118

77

59

65

MELTING POINT BOILING POINT DENSITY

ATOMIC MASS
167.259

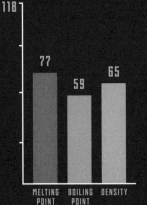

THULIUM

STATE AT 20°C

A bright, silvery metal.

WHERE ON EARTH?

Found mainly in the mineral monazite.

DANGER TO LIFE

No known biological role.
It is non-toxic.

SPECIAL USES

Portable X-ray machines,
cables, lasers.

THE VIKING

DISCOVERED IN 1879

The least abundant lanthanide, thulium occurs in small quantities in a number of minerals. It is named after Thule, the ancient name of a region close to modern-day Scandinavia, home of the Vikings. Thulium is too expensive to have many commercial uses, but thulium lasers exist. It is also used in imaging sensors. Thulium lasers are also used in some surgical procedures and the element acts as a radioactive source in portable X-ray machines.

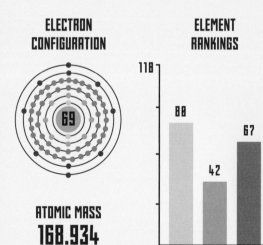

ELECTRON CONFIGURATION

69

ATOMIC MASS
168.934

ELEMENT RANKINGS

118

80

42

67

MELTING POINT   BOILING POINT   DENSITY

YTTERBIUM

Yb

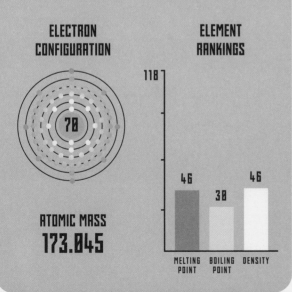

STATE AT 20°C
A soft, silvery metal.

WHERE ON EARTH?
Found mainly in the mineral monazite.

DANGER TO LIFE
No known biological role. It has low toxicity.

SPECIAL USES
Memory devices, lasers, glass.

THE MINER

 DISCOVERED IN 1878

The town of Ytterby in Sweden is home to an infamous mine in which many elements were discovered. Ytterbium is named after it. The ores in which the elements were discovered were donated to chemists by the miners who worked there. Ytterbium atomic clocks are incredibly accurate timekeepers. They 'tick' 518 trillion times each second and could operate for as long as the Universe has been around – nearly 14 billion years – before they lost a second of time.

ELECTRON CONFIGURATION

70

ATOMIC MASS
173.045

ELEMENT RANKINGS

118

MELTING POINT 46
BOILING POINT 30
DENSITY 46

LUTETIUM

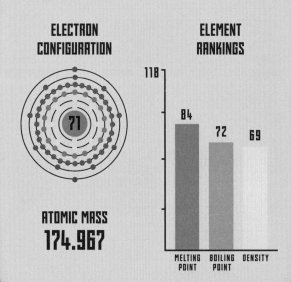

Lu

STATE AT 20°C
A hard, silvery-white metal.

WHERE ON EARTH?
Found mainly in the mineral monazite.

DANGER TO LIFE
No known biological role.
It has low toxicity.

SPECIAL USES
Limited use outside of research.

THE MONA LISA

 DISCOVERED IN 1907

The last natural rare earth element to be discovered, lutetium comes from *Lutetia*, the Latin word for Paris – the native city of its discoverer Georges Urbain and home of the *Mona Lisa*. (It was also discovered around the same time by Charles James in the USA and Karl Auer in Germany). Lutetium-176 decays incredibly slowly, with a half-life longer than the age of the Universe. Measuring its levels inside meteorites is a great way to tell their age.

ELECTRON CONFIGURATION

71

ATOMIC MASS
174.967

ELEMENT RANKINGS

118

84

72

69

MELTING POINT | BOILING POINT | DENSITY

HAFNIUM

ELECTRON CONFIGURATION

72

ATOMIC MASS
178.49

ELEMENT RANKINGS

118

94	88	81
MELTING POINT	BOILING POINT	DENSITY

STATE AT 20°C
A shiny, silvery metal.

WHERE ON EARTH?
Found in zirconium ores.

DANGER TO LIFE
No known biological role. It has low toxicity.

SPECIAL USES
Nuclear submarines, microchips, welding torches.

SPACE ROCKET

 DISCOVERED IN 1923

Although hafnium was first predicted by Dmitri Mendeleev in 1869, it was not isolated until 1923. It is commonly used in electronic equipment, but its resistance to corrosion and high melting point also make it useful for space rocket engines. Like its neighbour, lutetium, hafnium takes its name from the Latin form of a European capital city. This time it is Copenhagen (or *Hafnia*). It is rarely seen as a free element in nature and is often found in zirconium minerals.

TANTALUM

Ta

STATE AT 20°C
A shiny, silvery metal.

WHERE ON EARTH?
Found mainly in the mineral columbite-tantalite.

DANGER TO LIFE
No known biological role. It is non-toxic.

SPECIAL USES
Artificial joints, dental implants, neon lights.

ELECTRIC FRUIT

DISCOVERED IN 1802

Due to its close proximity to niobium in the periodic table, tantalum is named after her father, *Tantalus*, the Greek god who was forced to stand beneath a tree bearing low-hanging fruit for all eternity. Tantalum is frequently used in the production of electronic components, particularly mobile phones and games consoles. Its not recognised as a threat by the immune system which makes it particularly ideal for surgical instruments and implants.

ELECTRON CONFIGURATION

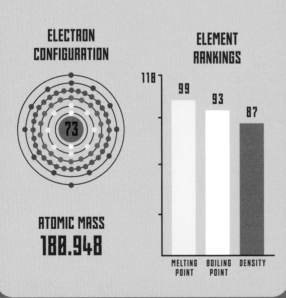

73

ATOMIC MASS
180.948

ELEMENT RANKINGS

118

MELTING POINT	BOILING POINT	DENSITY
99	93	87

TUNGSTEN

STATE AT 20°C
A shiny, silvery-white metal.

WHERE ON EARTH?
Found in the ores scheelite and wolframite.

DANGER TO LIFE
Limited biological role; used by some bacteria.

SPECIAL USES
Cutting and drilling tools, dentistry, fluorescent lighting.

BIG BAD WOLF

 DISCOVERED IN 1783

One of the toughest elements, with the highest melting point of any metal, tungsten's name comes from the Swedish words *tung* and *sten* meaning 'heavy stone'. Due to its strength and resistance to corrosion, tungsten is often used to harden saw blades or make drill bits. It also forms the filament inside many types of light bulb. Tungsten's chemical symbol – W – comes from the German word *wolfram*, meaning 'wolf'.

ELECTRON CONFIGURATION

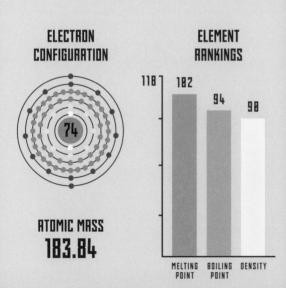

74

ATOMIC MASS
183.84

ELEMENT RANKINGS

118

MELTING POINT	BOILING POINT	DENSITY
102	94	90

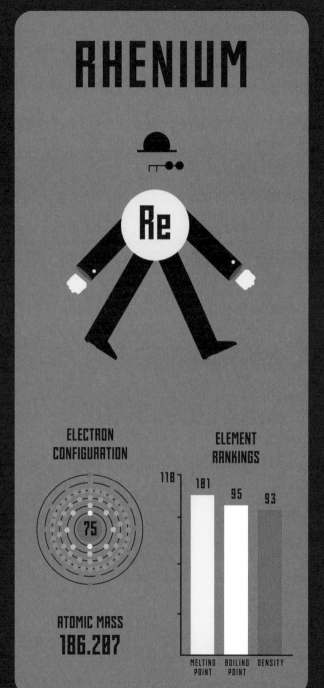

RHENIUM

Re

ELECTRON CONFIGURATION

75

ATOMIC MASS
186.207

ELEMENT RANKINGS

118

101	95	93
MELTING POINT	BOILING POINT	DENSITY

STATE AT 20°C
A heavy, silvery-grey metal.

WHERE ON EARTH?
Not found in mineable minerals but in the Earth's crust.

DANGER TO LIFE
No known biological role. Exposure may cause respiratory problems and skin irritation.

SPECIAL USES
Oven filaments, X-ray machines, turbine blades.

MR INVISIBLE

 DISCOVERED IN 1925

Chemically similar to manganese and technetium, rhenium was one of the last elements to be discovered with a stable isotope. It took several attempts to find it after Mendeleev predicted its existence, so in some ways it can be thought of as 'the invisible element'. It takes its name from the Rhine, the second longest river in Western Europe. It is used in jet engine blades and nozzles.

OSMIUM

Os

ELECTRON CONFIGURATION

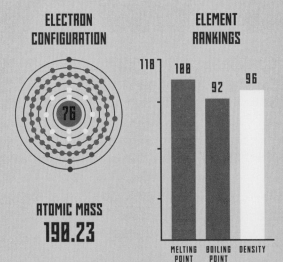

76

ATOMIC MASS
190.23

ELEMENT RANKINGS

118

100

92

96

MELTING POINT · BOILING POINT · DENSITY

STATE AT 20°C
A shiny, bluish-grey metal that resists corrosion.

WHERE ON EARTH?
Found in the mineral osmiridium.

DANGER TO LIFE
No known biological role. Its oxide is very toxic.

SPECIAL USES
Instrument pivots, needles, electrical contacts.

THE PACEMAKER

 DISCOVERED IN 1803

Osmium is a very versatile element often found near meteorite impact craters. It is the densest of all the naturally occurring elements, almost twice as dense as lead, and is often found alloyed to nickel and copper. Platinum-osmium alloys are frequently used in pacemakers and replacement heart valves. Osmiridium – an alloy of osmium and iridium – is used in fountain pens nibs and the needles for vinyl record players.

IRIDIUM

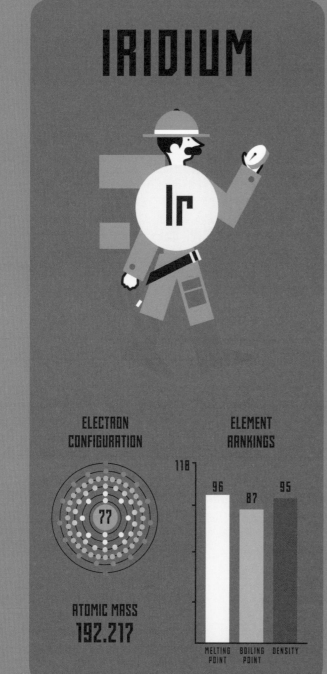

Ir

STATE AT 20°C
A hard, silvery, unreactive, metal.

WHERE ON EARTH?
Found in sediments deposited by rivers.

DANGER TO LIFE
No known biological role. It has low toxicity.

SPECIAL USES
Pen tips, compass bearings, spark plugs.

ELECTRON CONFIGURATION

77

ATOMIC MASS
192.217

ELEMENT RANKINGS

118

96 | 87 | 95

MELTING POINT | BOILING POINT | DENSITY

DINOS' DEMISE

 DISCOVERED IN 1803

Geologists point to a thin layer of iridium-rich clay between rock layers under the Earth's surface as a key piece of evidence for the event that wiped out the dinosaurs. Iridium is rare on Earth, but far more abundant in asteroids, suggesting an asteroid strike could have been the cause of their sudden demise. Due to the range of colours of its salts, iridium gets its name from the Greek goddess Iris, who personifies the rainbow.

PLATINUM

STATE AT 20°C
A shiny, silvery-white metal that resists corrosion.

WHERE ON EARTH?
Found in the mineral cooperite (platinum sulfide).

DANGER TO LIFE
No known biological role. It is non-toxic.

SPECIAL USES
Catalytic converters for vehicles, computer hard disks, spark plugs.

FLASH GNASHERS

 DISCOVERED IN ANCIENT TIMES

Derived from the Spanish word *platino*, meaning 'little silver' platinum was first brought to Europe by Spanish explorers in the 18th century, although it had been used by humans for thousands of years before. Popular in jewellery manufacturing, platinum is also useful for dental fillings to provide strength and durability as it is one of the least reactive metals. Rarer and less commonly mined than gold, platinum is expensive to source and is considered a precious metal.

ELECTRON CONFIGURATION

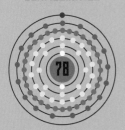
78

ATOMIC MASS
195.084

ELEMENT RANKINGS

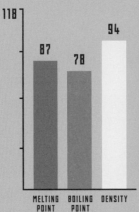

118

87
78
94

MELTING POINT | BOILING POINT | DENSITY

GOLD

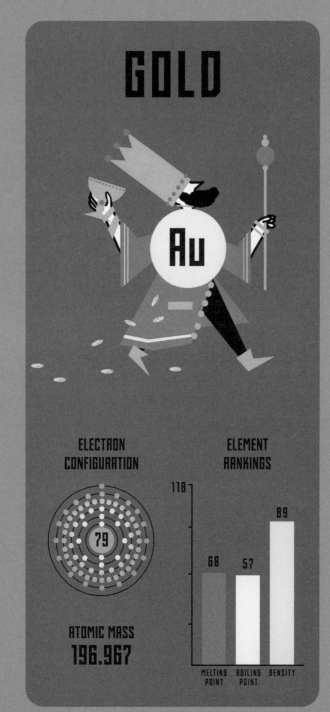

Au

STATE AT 20°C
A yellow, soft, unreactive metal.

WHERE ON EARTH?
Found in seawater and mined from mineral deposits.

DANGER TO LIFE
No known biological role. It is non-toxic.

SPECIAL USES
Jewellery, bullion, dental fillings, money, artificial limb joints.

ELECTRON CONFIGURATION

79

ATOMIC MASS
196.967

ELEMENT RANKINGS

118

89

68   57

MELTING POINT   BOILING POINT   DENSITY

FIT FOR A KING

 ## DISCOVERED IN ANCIENT TIMES

One of the most desirable metals, gold is a rare, naturally-occurring element with extremely dense and largely unreactive properties. Gold has been known since antiquity, with accounts of its usage documented across many civilisations. It is frequently associated with royalty and wealth. It is thought all gold on Earth was deposited via meteorites, and much of it sunk to our planet's core during its early formation. Its symbol – Au – comes from *aurum*, the Latin word for gold.

MERCURY

Hg

STATE AT 20°C
A liquid, silvery metal.

WHERE ON EARTH?
Found in cinnabar ores (mercury sulfide).

DANGER TO LIFE
No known biological role. It is toxic in high doses.

SPECIAL USES
Its use is slowly being phased out due to its high toxicity.

ELECTRON CONFIGURATION

80

ATOMIC MASS
200.592

ELEMENT RANKINGS

118

83

12

16

MELTING POINT | BOILING POINT | DENSITY

TOXIC LEVELS

 DISCOVERED IN ANCIENT TIMES

Mercury is the only metal liquid at standard temperature, the result of weak bonds in its atomic make-up. A poor conductor of heat, mercury can withstand high temperatures, making it ideally suited for thermometers. Its high levels of toxicity mean that its usage for consumer products is being phased out, although it is useful for many things including insecticides, wood preservatives and fluorescent light bulbs. Mercury is named after the Roman messenger god.

THALLIUM

ELECTRON CONFIGURATION

81

ATOMIC MASS
204.38

ELEMENT RANKINGS

118

76

33

38

MELTING POINT | BOILING POINT | DENSITY

STATE AT 20°C
A soft, silvery-white metal that tarnishes easily in air.

WHERE ON EARTH?
Found in several ores such as pyrites and on the ocean floor.

DANGER TO LIFE
No known biological role. It is very toxic.

SPECIAL USES
Limited use due to its toxicity.

NIGHT GOGGLES

 DISCOVERED IN 1861

Thallium is named after the Greek word *thallos*, meaning 'green shoot' or 'twig'. When electrons in a thallium atom drop down to a lower shell they give off a characteristic green light. Thallium has a low melting point, making it ideal for special glass and highly reflective lenses. It's particularly good for infrared optics. However, it's extremely toxic to humans and can cause fatal thallium poisoning. At one point it was also used as rat poison and ant killer.

LEAD

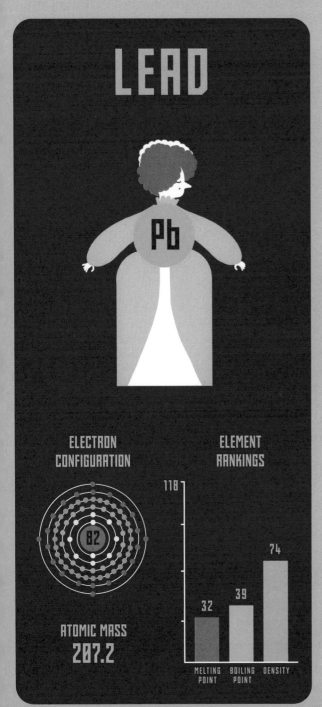

Pb

ELECTRON CONFIGURATION

82

ATOMIC MASS
207.2

ELEMENT RANKINGS

118

74

39

32

MELTING POINT | BOILING POINT | DENSITY

STATE AT 20°C
A dull, silvery-grey metal.

WHERE ON EARTH?
Found mainly in the mineral galena.

DANGER TO LIFE
No known biological role.
It is toxic and carcinogenic.

SPECIAL USES
Car batteries, weight belts for diving, pigments, ammunition.

QUEEN OF LEAD
 ## DISCOVERED IN ANCIENT TIMES

We've known about this soft, malleable and dull metal since antiquity. Some of the earliest lead artefacts date back over 8,000 years. It was known to the Romans by the Latin word *plumbum,* meaning 'liquid silver', from which the element's symbol (Pb) and the word 'plumbing' originate. Unfortunately, we haven't always been aware of lead's toxic attributes. It is widely believed to have contributed to the death of Queen Elizabeth I, who used a fashionable lead-based white powder as makeup.

BISMUTH

Bi

STATE AT 20°C
A silvery, pink-tinged brittle metal.

WHERE ON EARTH?
Found in ores such as bismuthinite and bismite.

DANGER TO LIFE
No known biological role. It is non-toxic.

SPECIAL USES
Paints, fire detectors, fire extinguishers, electric fuses.

SHIMMER EYE

 DISCOVERED IN APPROX. 1500

This pink-tinged element is the most diamagnetic of all metals, meaning it is strongly repelled by a magnetic field. It also has a high electrical resistance. Bismuth produces a shimmery, pearl-like powder which sticks well to skin, so it is often found in cosmetic products such as eye shadow and nail polish. You'll also find a bismuth alloy in many fire sprinkler systems. Its proximity to lead in the periodic table makes it a good substitute for its poisonous neighbour.

ELECTRON CONFIGURATION

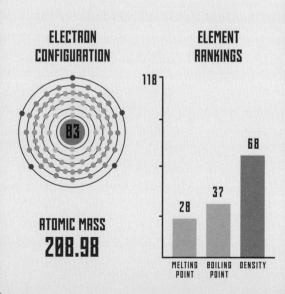

83

ATOMIC MASS
208.98

ELEMENT RANKINGS

118

28	37	68
MELTING POINT	BOILING POINT	DENSITY

POLONIUM

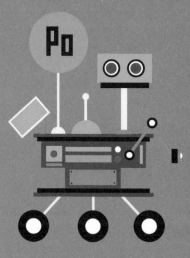

Po

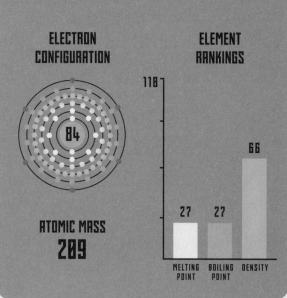

STATE AT 20°C
A silvery-grey, radioactive semi-metal.

WHERE ON EARTH?
Found in uranium ores, it is a very rare natural element.

DANGER TO LIFE
No known biological role. It is radioactive and highly toxic.

SPECIAL USES
Antistatic devices, space equipment, research.

MARS ROVER

 DISCOVERED IN 1898

Named after Poland, polonium is highly unstable, radioactive and toxic. An amount less than the size of a full stop contains more than 3,000 times the lethal dosage for humans. In 2006 a former Russian spy called Alexander Litvinenko was murdered by secret agents using polonium. Polonium is also found in tobacco smoke, just one of the reasons smoking is dangerous. Polonium is safe to use in space far from any people and is used to heat lunar and Mars rovers.

ELECTRON CONFIGURATION

84

ATOMIC MASS
209

ELEMENT RANKINGS

118

MELTING POINT	BOILING POINT	DENSITY
27	27	66

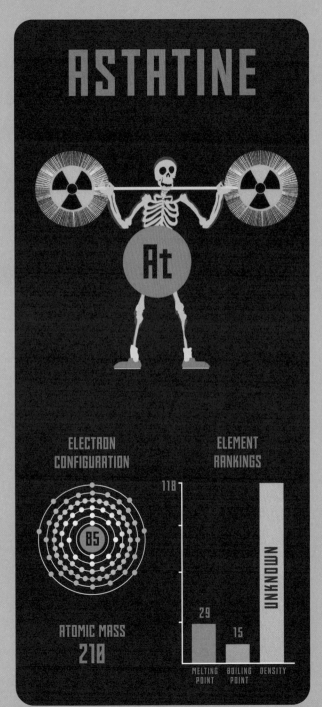

ASTATINE

At

ELECTRON
CONFIGURATION

85

ATOMIC MASS
210

ELEMENT
RANKINGS

118

29

MELTING
POINT

15

BOILING
POINT

UNKNOWN

DENSITY

STATE AT 20°C
A radioactive element,
not seen by the naked eye.

WHERE ON EARTH?
The rarest naturally occurring
element in the Earth's crust.

DANGER TO LIFE
No known biological role.
It is radioactive and highly toxic.

SPECIAL USES
No uses outside of scientific
research.

DEADLY OGRE

 DISCOVERED IN 1940

Dangerously radioactive, astatine has
no uses outside of scientific research
and to this day very little is known
about it. It is the rarest naturally-
occurring element in the Earth's
crust. Even the most stable of its 39
isotopes has a half-life of just eight
hours. Mendeleev speculated about its
existence when he began creating his
version of the periodic table and it's
only from its position in the table that
we can guess at its properties.

RADON

Rn

STATE AT 20°C
A colourless and odourless gas.

WHERE ON EARTH?
Naturally produced from the decay of elements in the Earth's crust.

DANGER TO LIFE
No known biological role.
It is highly toxic.

SPECIAL USES
Limited use due to its radioactivity.

HOT WATER
DISCOVERED IN 1900

Radon is a naturally occurring, highly toxic and radioactive gas produced as a by-product of decaying elements in the Earth's crust, including radium, uranium and thorium. It has even been found in groundwater and hot springs. Radon is considered a major health hazard – in the USA alone 21,000 deaths per year are attributed to lung cancer brought on by exposure to radon. That said, used in the right way, it can also be an effective cancer treatment as radiotherapy.

ELECTRON CONFIGURATION

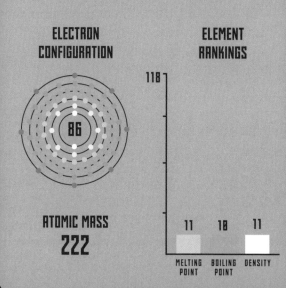

86

ATOMIC MASS
222

ELEMENT RANKINGS

118

MELTING POINT	BOILING POINT	DENSITY
11	18	11

FRANCIUM

STATE AT 20°C
A radioactive element, not seen by the naked eye.

WHERE ON EARTH?
Found in uranium and thorium ores.

DANGER TO LIFE
No known biological role. It is radioactive and highly toxic.

SPECIAL USES
No uses outside of scientific research.

GO FRANCE!

DISCOVERED IN 1939

Incredibly rare, with a maximum half-life of just 22 minutes, little is known about the element named after the country of its discoverer Marguerite Perey. The most unstable of all naturally-occurring elements, no more than 30 grams are present in the Earth's crust at any one time. The largest amount created in a laboratory is just 300,000 atoms (compared to about five sextillion atoms in a single drop of water, which is written as 5,000,000,000,000,000,000,000).

ELECTRON CONFIGURATION

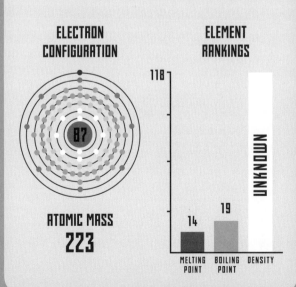

87

ATOMIC MASS
223

ELEMENT RANKINGS

118

14
MELTING POINT

19
BOILING POINT

UNKNOWN
DENSITY

RADIUM

STATE AT 20°C
A bright white reactive metal.

WHERE ON EARTH?
Found in uranium ores.

DANGER TO LIFE
No known biological role.
It is radioactive and highly toxic.

SPECIAL USES
Limited use due to its radioactivity.

ELECTRON CONFIGURATION

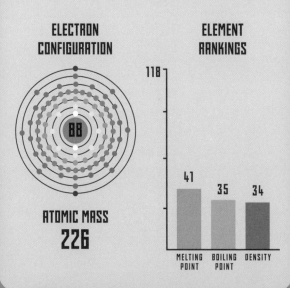

88

ATOMIC MASS
226

ELEMENT RANKINGS

118

41
35
34

MELTING POINT | BOILING POINT | DENSITY

DEAD IN TIME
DISCOVERED IN 1898

Discovered only a few months after the discovery of polonium in 1898, radium is a bright white metal that quickly turns black and tarnishes in air. Highly reactive and extremely dangerous, radium was once used for many commercial objects, including wristwatches, toothpaste and paint. Its radiant glow was useful for objects which needed to be visible in the dark, but its usage in factories contributed to the deaths of many workers and the practice was ceased.

ACTINIUM

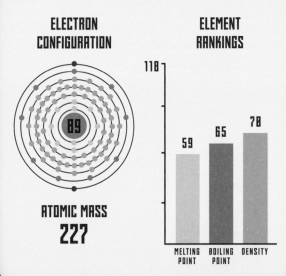

ELECTRON CONFIGURATION

89

ATOMIC MASS
227

ELEMENT RANKINGS

118

59	65	70
MELTING POINT	BOILING POINT	DENSITY

STATE AT 20°C
A soft, silvery-white metal which glows blue in the dark.

WHERE ON EARTH?
Found in uranium ores.

DANGER TO LIFE
No known biological role. It is radioactive and highly toxic.

SPECIAL USES
Limited use outside of research.

ALPHA-GLOW

 DISCOVERED IN 1899

Another extremely rare element, actinium is hardly used outside of research. It glows pale blue in the dark and its name comes from the Greek word *aktinos*, meaning 'beam' or 'ray', because it is a powerful source of alpha radiation. In turn, it gives its name to the actinides series of elements and is the first member of that group. It has a potential use in cancer treatment and is also used in a probe that can measure the water content of soil.

THORIUM

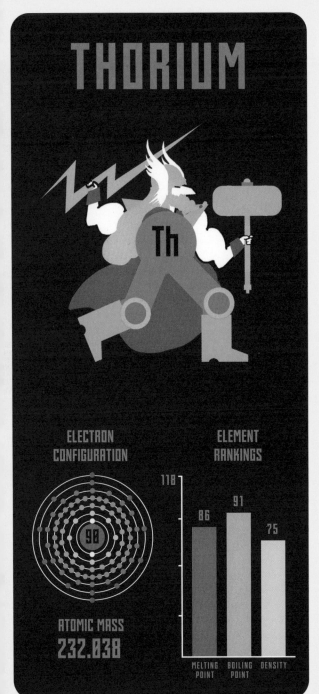

ELECTRON CONFIGURATION

90

ATOMIC MASS
232.038

ELEMENT RANKINGS

118

86 — MELTING POINT
91 — BOILING POINT
75 — DENSITY

STATE AT 20°C
A silvery, radioactive metal.

WHERE ON EARTH?
Found in the minerals thorite, thorianite and monazite.

DANGER TO LIFE
No known biological role.
It is radioactive and highly toxic.

SPECIAL USES
Nuclear power, high-quality camera lenses.

GREAT GODS

 DISCOVERED IN 1829

Named after Thor, the Norse god of war and thunder, thorium is used as a nuclear power source as it is slightly radioactive. The half-life of its most common form is about the same as the age of the Universe. When used as an alloying agent, thorium gives other metals great strength and increased resistance to high temperatures. It can be found in trace amounts in most rocks and soils.

PROTACTINIUM

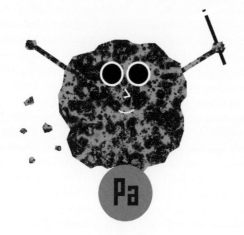

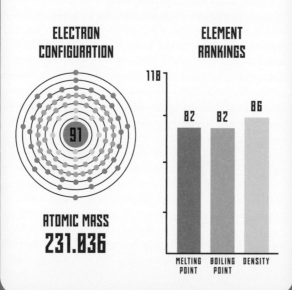

Pa

ELECTRON CONFIGURATION

91

ATOMIC MASS
231.036

ELEMENT RANKINGS

110

MELTING POINT	BOILING POINT	DENSITY
82	82	86

STATE AT 20°C
A silvery-grey, radioactive metal.

WHERE ON EARTH?
Found in uranium ores and ocean sediments.

DANGER TO LIFE
No known biological role.
It is radioactive and highly toxic.

SPECIAL USES
Limited use outside of research.

PROTO-ELEMENT

 ## DISCOVERED IN 1913

The radioactive decay of uranium produces protactinium, which in turn decays into actinium. The beginning of this element's name reflects just that, from the Greek word *proto* meaning 'before' actinium. A silvery-grey, radioactive metal, protactinium is one of the rarest and most expensive naturally-occurring elements. Its presence in ocean sediments has allowed geologists to work out how the sea changed during the last ice age.

URANIUM

ELECTRON CONFIGURATION

92

ATOMIC MASS
238.029

ELEMENT RANKINGS

118

66 — MELTING POINT
83 — BOILING POINT
88 — DENSITY

STATE AT 20°C
A silvery, radioactive metal.

WHERE ON EARTH?
Found in minerals such as uraninite, brannerite and carnotite.

DANGER TO LIFE
No known biological role.
It is toxic.

SPECIAL USES
Nuclear fuel, armour, ammunition, ballast for ships.

SUPER POWER
DISCOVERED IN 1789

This naturally-occurring radioactive element is fairly common in the Earth's crust and can be found almost anywhere including in soils, rocks, freshwater and saltwater. About 11 per cent of the world's electricity is currently generated by nuclear power stations fuelled by the radioactive decay of uranium. It is also used in nuclear submarines and nuclear weapons. It takes its name from the planet Uranus.

NEPTUNIUM

Np

ELECTRON CONFIGURATION

93

ATOMIC MASS
237

ELEMENT RANKINGS

118

92

88

38

MELTING POINT | BOILING POINT | DENSITY

STATE AT 20°C
A silvery metallic radioactive metal.

WHERE ON EARTH?
Trace amounts found in uranium ores.

DANGER TO LIFE
No known biological role. It is radioactive and highly toxic.

SPECIAL USES
Limited use outside of research.

FIRE STARTER

 DISCOVERED IN 1940

Named after the planet Neptune, this radioactive metal is capable of spontaneously catching fire at room temperature. It's the first so-called transuranic element – those with atomic numbers higher than uranium. As a general rule, transuranic elements are radioactive, rare or absent in nature and have half-lifes shorter than the age of the Earth (4.56 billion years). Neptunium is a by-product of americium decay, which is found in smoke detectors.

PLUTONIUM

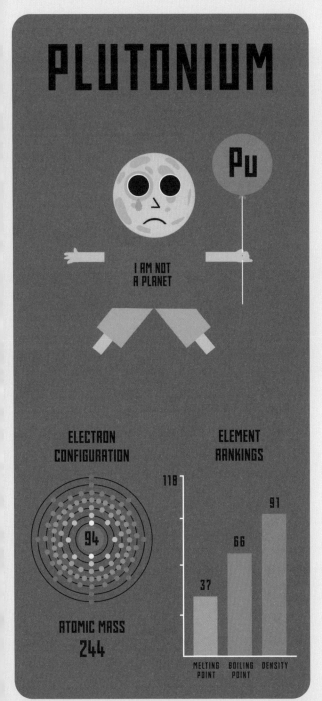

Pu

I AM NOT
A PLANET

STATE AT 20°C
A silvery, radioactive metal.

WHERE ON EARTH?
Manufactured by the irradiation of uranium in nuclear reactors.

DANGER TO LIFE
No known biological role.
It is radioactive and highly toxic.

SPECIAL USES
Nuclear weapons, nuclear power, space fuel.

ROBOT FUEL

 DISCOVERED IN 1940

Named after Pluto, plutonium was found ten years after the dwarf planet was discovered in 1930. Its space-themed name is very apt because plutonium is now used as a radioactive fuel source for robotic spacecraft, including NASA's New Horizons mission that visited Pluto in 2015. In the past, it was also used in the development of nuclear power and in the atomic bomb dropped on the Japanese city of Nagasaki in August 1945.

ELECTRON CONFIGURATION

94

ATOMIC MASS
244

ELEMENT RANKINGS

118

91

66

37

MELTING POINT | BOILING POINT | DENSITY

94

AMERICIUM

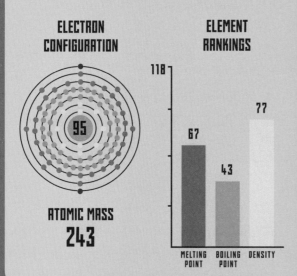

ELECTRON CONFIGURATION

95

ATOMIC MASS
243

ELEMENT RANKINGS

118

67
43
77

MELTING POINT | BOILING POINT | DENSITY

STATE AT 20°C
A shiny, silvery radioactive metal.

WHERE ON EARTH?
Trace amounts found in uranium minerals.

DANGER TO LIFE
No known biological role. It is radioactive and highly toxic.

SPECIAL USES
Smoke alarms, spacecraft, batteries of the future.

SPACE LIBERTY

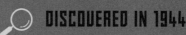

DISCOVERED IN 1944

Americium is named after the Americas. A radioactive metal, it is frequently used in smoke detectors in the form of americium dioxide. Smoke entering the detector absorbs the alpha particles emitted by americium, changing the way the electric current flows inside and triggering the alarm. Like its neighbour plutonium, it might be used in future space travel instead of solar panels for missions too far from the Sun.

CURIUM

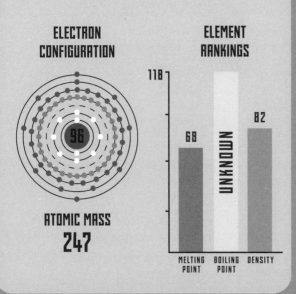

STATE AT 20°C
A silvery-white radioactive metal.

WHERE ON EARTH?
May be found in natural deposits of uranium; made in a nuclear reactor.

DANGER TO LIFE
No known biological role.
It is radioactive and highly toxic.

SPECIAL USES
Powers electrical equipment used on space missions.

SUPER-DUO

 DISCOVERED IN 1944

Curium is a silvery-white metal named after husband and wife super-duo Pierre and Marie Curie, who carried out pioneering work on radioactivity. It has been used on Mars rovers as a source of alpha particles in devices that examine what Martian rocks are made of. It's also a by-product of using uranium and plutonium in nuclear power stations. Every tonne of used nuclear fuel contains about twenty grams of curium.

ELECTRON CONFIGURATION

96

ATOMIC MASS
247

ELEMENT RANKINGS

118

69

UNKNOWN

82

MELTING POINT | BOILING POINT | DENSITY

BERKELIUM

Bk

STATE AT 20°C
A silvery, radioactive metal.

WHERE ON EARTH?
Manufactured by the neutron bombardment of plutonium-239.

DANGER TO LIFE
No known biological role.
It is radioactive and highly toxic.

SPECIAL USES
Limited use outside of research.

HEAVY TARGET

 DISCOVERED IN 1949

This element is named after the Lawrence Berkeley National Laboratory located in the city of Berkeley, California, USA – a place with a long history of protests, including for civil rights and against the Vietnam War. Berkelium is artificially produced, and has only been made in small amounts. It was first discovered by bombarding americium-241 with an alpha particle. Today, it is mostly used as a target inside cyclotrons in order to create even heavier elements.

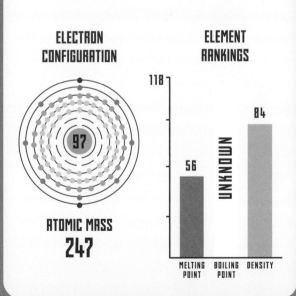

ELECTRON CONFIGURATION

97

ATOMIC MASS
247

ELEMENT RANKINGS

118

56

84

UNKNOWN

MELTING POINT | BOILING POINT | DENSITY

CALIFORNIUM

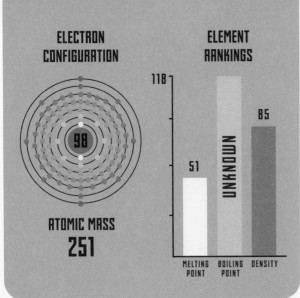

STATE AT 20°C
A radioactive metal.

WHERE ON EARTH?
Manufactured by neutron bombardment of plutonium-239.

DANGER TO LIFE
No known biological role.
It is radioactive and highly toxic.

SPECIAL USES
Portable metal detectors.

ELECTRON CONFIGURATION

98

ATOMIC MASS
251

ELEMENT RANKINGS

118

85

51

UNKNOWN

MELTING POINT | BOILING POINT | DENSITY

GO CALIFORNIA!

 DISCOVERED IN 1950

Also discovered at Berkeley, californium is an extremely radioactive element. It is very good at producing neutrons. A single gram of californium produces two trillion neutrons a second. Neutrons from californium have been used in the treatment of cervical and brain cancers. Californium-produced neutrons are also fired at aircraft to search for any defects or damage that could pose a safety threat. Californium has to be handled very carefully as it can affect the body's ability to make red blood cells.

EINSTEINIUM

Es

ELECTRON CONFIGURATION

99

ATOMIC MASS
252

ELEMENT RANKINGS

118

50 | UNKNOWN | UNKNOWN

MELTING POINT | BOILING POINT | DENSITY

STATE AT 20°C
A radioactive metal.

WHERE ON EARTH?
Manufactured by bombardment of plutonium in a nuclear reactor.

DANGER TO LIFE
No known biological role. It is radioactive and highly toxic.

SPECIAL USES
No uses outside of scientific research.

TOP SECRET

DISCOVERED IN 1952

Einsteinium was discovered in 1952 and named in honour of Albert Einstein, but its discovery was kept secret until 1955 due to the Cold War. It was originally discovered amongst the debris left over from a hydrogen bomb test and has no use outside of scientific research. Extremely radioactive, only a few milligrams of this substance are made each year. Its decay creates so much energy that a sample of einsteinium emits a visible glow.

FERMIUM

STATE AT 20°C
A radioactive metal.

WHERE ON EARTH?
Manufactured by bombardment of plutonium in a nuclear reactor.

DANGER TO LIFE
No known biological role.
It is radioactive and highly toxic.

SPECIAL USES
No uses outside of scientific research.

THREE DIGITS

DISCOVERED IN 1953

We're now into the elements with three-digit atomic numbers! Fermium was discovered in 1953 at the Lawrence Berkeley National Laboratory. It takes its name from Italian physicist Enrico Fermi, a Nobel prize winner who designed the world's first nuclear reactor. He died the year that the discovery was made public. Such small amounts of the element have been produced that very little is known about it other than it is highly radioactive and has a very short half-life.

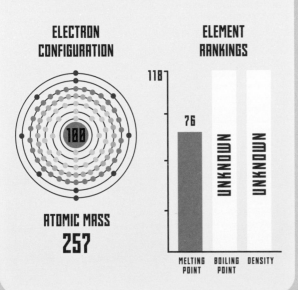

ELECTRON CONFIGURATION

100

ATOMIC MASS
257

ELEMENT RANKINGS

118

76

MELTING POINT

UNKNOWN
BOILING POINT

UNKNOWN
DENSITY

MENDELEVIUM

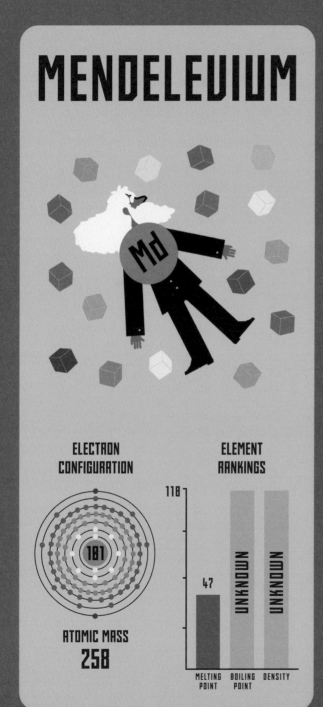

STATE AT 20°C
A radioactive metal.

WHERE ON EARTH?
Manufactured by bombarding einsteinium with alpha particles.

DANGER TO LIFE
No known biological role.

SPECIAL USES
No uses outside of scientific research.

ELECTRON CONFIGURATION

101

ATOMIC MASS
258

ELEMENT RANKINGS

118

47

UNKNOWN

UNKNOWN

MELTING POINT | BOILING POINT | DENSITY

THE FOUNDER

DISCOVERED IN 1955

Named after Dmitri Mendeleev, only a limited number of mendelevium atoms have ever been made. It was first synthesised by bombarding a billion Einsteinium atoms with alpha particles, which produced just seventeen atoms of mendelevium. Discovered during the Cold War, it was a brave move for an American team to name an element after a Russian scientist. In fact, Glenn Seaborg had to seek the permission of the US government before announcing the new name.

NOBELIUM

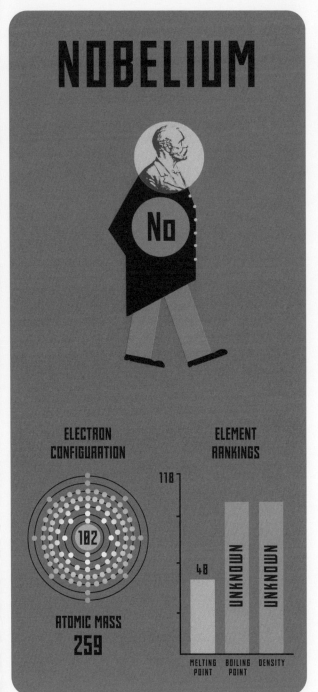

STATE AT 20°C
A radioactive metal.

WHERE ON EARTH?
Manufactured by bombarding curium with carbon.

DANGER TO LIFE
No known biological role.
It is radioactive and highly toxic.

SPECIAL USES
No uses outside of scientific research.

ELECTRON CONFIGURATION

102

ATOMIC MASS
259

ELEMENT RANKINGS

118

MELTING POINT: 48
BOILING POINT: UNKNOWN
DENSITY: UNKNOWN

NOT SO JOLLY

 ## DISCOVERED IN 1963

Nobelium is named after the Swedish scientist Alfred Nobel, creator of the Nobel prizes and inventor of dynamite. The Joint Institute of Nuclear Research in Russia is officially credited with its discovery in 1963, although this has been disputed by several research teams. Nobelium's most stable isotope has a half-life of just 58 minutes. Firing three trillion carbon-12 atoms a second at a target of californium-249 for ten minutes produces around 1,000 nobelium-255 atoms.

LAWRENCIUM

STATE AT 20°C
A radioactive metal.

WHERE ON EARTH?
Manufactured by bombarding californium with boron.

DANGER TO LIFE
No known biological role.

SPECIAL USES
No uses outside of scientific research.

CYCLOTRONIC
DISCOVERED IN 1965

Lawrencium is named after American nuclear physicist Ernest Lawrence, the inventor of the cyclotron – a piece of scientific equipment instrumental in the discovery of many of the heaviest elements in the periodic table. Lawrencium was discovered three years after his death and is the final member of the actinide series. Its most stable isotope is lawrencium-266, which has a half-life of eleven hours. There has been a heated debate about whether it was discovered in the USA or Russia.

ELECTRON CONFIGURATION

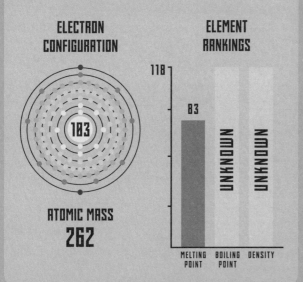

103

ATOMIC MASS
262

ELEMENT RANKINGS

118

83

UNKNOWN

UNKNOWN

MELTING POINT | BOILING POINT | DENSITY

RUTHERFORDIUM

STATE AT 20°C
A radioactive metal.

WHERE ON EARTH?
Manufactured by bombarding californium-249 with carbon-12.

DANGER TO LIFE
No known biological role.

SPECIAL USES
Limited use outside of scientific research.

ATOM FINDER

 DISCOVERED IN 1964

Rutherfordium is named after New Zealand-born physicist Ernest Rutherford, one of the first scientists to explain the structure of atoms. Joint credit has been given to American and Russian teams for its discovery. The Russians had suggested the name kurchatovium, after their former head of Soviet nuclear research, Igor Kurchatov. However, rutherfordium eventually won out. It has few practical uses beyond scientific research.

ELECTRON CONFIGURATION

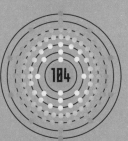

104

ATOMIC MASS
267

ELEMENT RANKINGS

118

UNKNOWN | UNKNOWN | UNKNOWN

MELTING POINT | BOILING POINT | DENSITY

DUBNIUM

Db

STATE AT 20°C
A highly radioactive metal.

WHERE ON EARTH?
Manufactured by bombarding californium-249 with nitrogen-15.

DANGER TO LIFE
No known biological role.

SPECIAL USES
No uses outside of scientific research.

ELECTRON CONFIGURATION

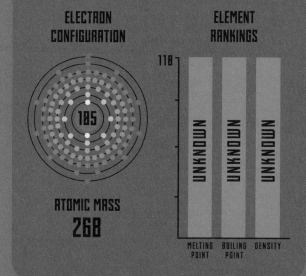

105

ATOMIC MASS
268

ELEMENT RANKINGS

118

UNKNOWN | UNKNOWN | UNKNOWN

MELTING POINT | BOILING POINT | DENSITY

COLD WAR

DISCOVERED IN 1968–1970

As with the previous elements, the discovery of dubnium has been long argued. This fierce battle between the USA and the former Soviet Union became known as the Transfermium Wars. This time the Russians won the race to name the new element, calling it dubnium after the town of Dubna, home to the Joint Institute for Nuclear Research. Other names had been suggested, including joliotium (after Frédéric Joliot-Curie) and hahnium (after Otto Hahn).

SEABORGIUM

STATE AT 20°C
A radioactive metal.

WHERE ON EARTH?
Manufactured by bombarding californium-249 with oxygen-18.

DANGER TO LIFE
No known biological role.

SPECIAL USES
No uses outside of scientific research.

MR POPULAR

 DISCOVERED IN 1974

There are only two elements named after people who were still alive at the time of discovery. The first is seaborgium, named after the American scientist Glenn Seaborg who played a significant role in the discovery of ten transuranic elements (elements with an atomic number higher than 92), including this one. There was a bit of controversy at the time about naming an element after a living person and an alternative was considered before bowing to significant public pressure.

ELECTRON CONFIGURATION

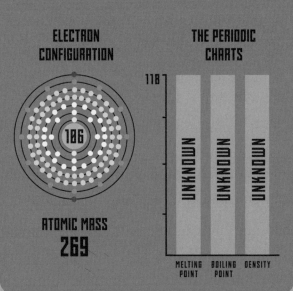

106

THE PERIODIC CHARTS

118

UNKNOWN | UNKNOWN | UNKNOWN

MELTING POINT | BOILING POINT | DENSITY

ATOMIC MASS
269

BOHRIUM

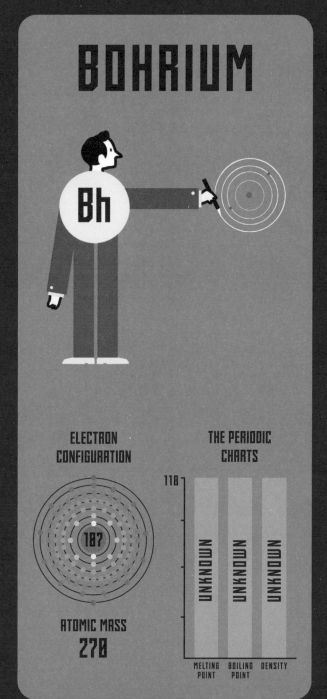

Bh

ELECTRON CONFIGURATION

107

ATOMIC MASS
270

THE PERIODIC CHARTS

118

MELTING POINT	BOILING POINT	DENSITY
UNKNOWN	UNKNOWN	UNKNOWN

STATE AT 20°C
A highly radioactive metal.

WHERE ON EARTH?
Manufactured by bombarding bismuth with atoms of chromium.

DANGER TO LIFE
No known biological role.

SPECIAL USES
No uses outside of scientific research.

TYPICAL STUFF

DISCOVERED IN 1981

Named after the influential Danish physicist Niels Bohr, bohrium's most stable confirmed isotope has a half-life of just one minute. The original suggestion for the element's name was nielsbohrium, but that was later shortened to bohrium because the first names of other scientists don't appear in the periodic table. Its most stable isotope – bohrium-278 – has a half-life of just 1.3 hours.

HASSIUM

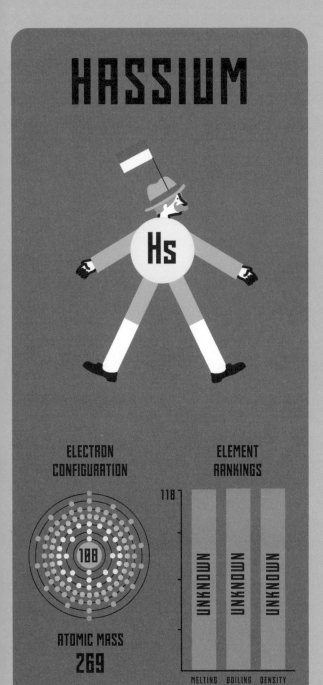

Hs

STATE AT 20°C
A highly radioactive metal.

WHERE ON EARTH?
Manufactured by bombarding lead with iron atoms.

DANGER TO LIFE
No known biological role.

SPECIAL USES
No uses outside of scientific research.

HEAVY RESEARCH

 DISCOVERED IN 1984

Hassium was named for the German state Hesse, which in Latin is *Hassia*. That's the location of the GSI Helmholtz Centre for Heavy Ion Research, a facility where hassium was discovered alongside bohrium, meitnerium, darmstadtium, roentgenium and copernicium. So far we've been able to establish that hassium behaves similarly to osmium, the element that sits above it in Group 8 of the periodic table. It has no stable isotopes and is still being investigated by scientists.

ELECTRON CONFIGURATION

108

ATOMIC MASS
269

ELEMENT RANKINGS

118

MELTING POINT	BOILING POINT	DENSITY
UNKNOWN	UNKNOWN	UNKNOWN

Elements 109–118 are a bit of mystery as they were only discovered between 1982 and 2004. They're super heavy (hence the heavy metal reference) and very unstable. Their names come from people and places, including the second living person to lend their name to an element (Yuri Oganessian and Oganesson) and the second woman to be honoured in the periodic table (Lise Meitner and Meitnerium).

It took a long time to decide some of these names, with lots of fighting between rival groups, so the elements were given unusual temporary names that reflected their atomic number. The five heaviest elements were originally called: ununquadium (114), ununpentium (115), ununhexium (116), ununseptium (117) and ununoctium (118). There might be more members of this group in the future as scientists continue to smash atoms together in the hunt for ever heavier elements. If we get to elements 122 and above then Glenn Seaborg suggested that we should call them the 'superactinide' series.

HEAVIES

Meitnerium [Mt]
Atomic number: 109
Atomic mass: 278

Darmstadtium [Ds]
Atomic number: 110
Atomic mass: 281

Roentgenium [Rg]
Atomic number: 111
Atomic mass: 280

Copernicium [Cn]
Atomic number: 112
Atomic mass: 285

Nihonium [Nh]
Atomic number: 113
Atomic mass: 286

Flerovium [Fl]
Atomic number: 114
Atomic mass: 289

Moscovium [Mc]
Atomic number: 115
Atomic mass: 289

Livermorium [Lv]
Atomic number: 116
Atomic mass: 293

Tennessine [Ts]
Atomic number: 117
Atomic mass: 294

Oganesson [Og]
Atomic number: 118
Atomic mass: 294

Element 119

From the outside it looks like a pretty average building nestled between the birch trees of Dubna, a town 125 kilometres north of Moscow, Russia. Yet what's happening inside its walls is remarkable. It is as this $60 million Superheavy Element Factory that the periodic table could get its next additions. Six machines are on the hunt for elements 119 and 120 by smashing light atoms into heavy ones using a giant magnet that weighs a thousand tonnes. The machine – called a cyclotron – produces six trillion atoms a second.

The facility is run by Yuri Oganessian, who lends his name to the heaviest element found so far. The discovery of Oganesson completed the seventh period of the periodic table. If he helps find any more then we'll have to start an eighth row. The last time a new row was needed was after the discovery of uranium in 1789. Discoveries like these don't come around every day.

However, what they're trying to do is far from easy. Element 118 was found by firing calcium-48 (with 20 protons) at californium (with 98). To do the same to discover the next element would require a lot of einsteinium (with 99 protons), but there's simply not enough of it in existence. So scientists at the Superheavy Element Factory are trying something new instead – firing titanium-50 (22 protons) at berkelium (97 protons) and californium in the hunt for elements 119 and 120.

The Island of Stability

We have come a long way since the ancient days when we made our first steps on the long road to becoming masters of the extraordinary elements. Today, elements completely unknown to our ancestors are used inside technology that would have seemed like magic to them. Imagine giving a cave-person a smartphone or taking an iron-age settler on an aeroplane.

But our element odyssey isn't over. We haven't been able to use the latest elements in any meaningful way yet because they are so unstable and disappear in less than a second. But what if there are new elements yet to be found that could stick around long enough to turn them into world-changing technology? Some chemists talk about 'The Island of Stability'. This is a new part of the table yet to be added, but one where the elements are long-lived and useful. If we can find and harness them, perhaps today's technology will look as a primitive to our descendants as our ancestors' does to us.

Our technological journey hasn't been without its drawbacks. Our constant consumption of the latest must-have gadgets is fast becoming a crisis. The Earth's natural supply of elements is running out. Burning fossil fuels – ancient elements trapped underground – is producing so much carbon dioxide that the planet is rapidly warming up.

The Elements and You

You have a lot in common with the world around you, even if you don't realise it. The human body is made up of 34 different elements, many of which you'll find in everyday objects.

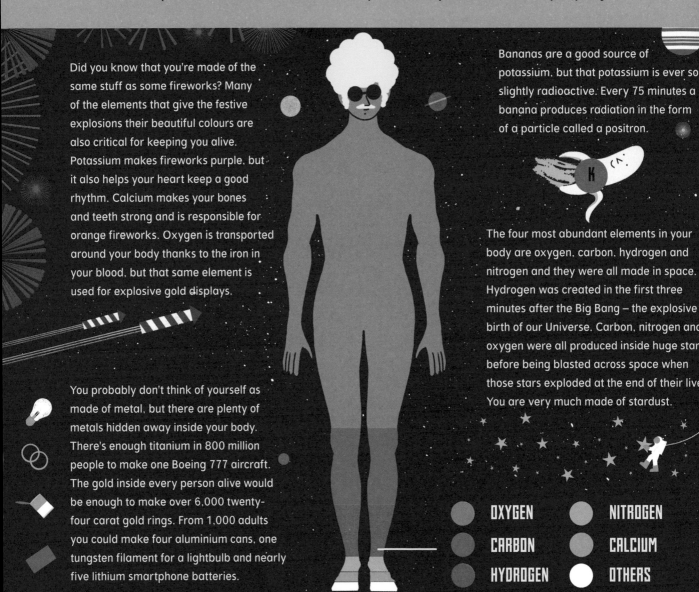

Did you know that you're made of the same stuff as some fireworks? Many of the elements that give the festive explosions their beautiful colours are also critical for keeping you alive. Potassium makes fireworks purple, but it also helps your heart keep a good rhythm. Calcium makes your bones and teeth strong and is responsible for orange fireworks. Oxygen is transported around your body thanks to the iron in your blood, but that same element is used for explosive gold displays.

You probably don't think of yourself as made of metal, but there are plenty of metals hidden away inside your body. There's enough titanium in 800 million people to make one Boeing 777 aircraft. The gold inside every person alive would be enough to make over 6,000 twenty-four carat gold rings. From 1,000 adults you could make four aluminium cans, one tungsten filament for a lightbulb and nearly five lithium smartphone batteries.

Bananas are a good source of potassium, but that potassium is ever so slightly radioactive. Every 75 minutes a banana produces radiation in the form of a particle called a positron.

The four most abundant elements in your body are oxygen, carbon, hydrogen and nitrogen and they were all made in space. Hydrogen was created in the first three minutes after the Big Bang – the explosive birth of our Universe. Carbon, nitrogen and oxygen were all produced inside huge stars before being blasted across space when those stars exploded at the end of their lives. You are very much made of stardust.

OXYGEN   NITROGEN

CARBON   CALCIUM

HYDROGEN   OTHERS

Elemental Olympics

We've seen in this book how each element has their own individual characteristics and personality. Here's a visual roundup of some of the most memorable comparisons.

OST REACTIVE:
FRANCIUM

LONGEST HALF LIFE:
TELLURIUM

LIGHTEST:
HYDROGEN

HEAVIEST:
OGANESSON

LOWEST BOILING POINT:
HELIUM

HIGHEST BOILING POINT:
TUNGSTEN

MOST EXPENSIVE:
CALIFORNIUM

GLOSSARY

A

acid – a chemical that when dissolved in water easily provides hydrogen ions.

atom – a tiny particle which makes up everything around you.

atomic mass – the average mass of an atom.

atomic number – the number of protons inside the nucleus of an atom.

B

boiling point – the temperature at which a liquid becomes a gas.

bond – the way in which atoms stick together to form a substance.

C

chemical – any substance that has been produced by changing atoms or molecules.

chemical reaction – a process in which the structure of a substance is changed.

chemical symbol – an abbreviation of a chemical element, represented as a one- or two-letter symbol.

compound – a molecule composed of two or more separate elements.

covalent bond – a chemical bond where electrons are shared between two atoms.

D

density – a measure of mass per unit of volume.

DNA – deoxyribonucleic acid, this is a molecule containing genetic information about a living thing.

E

electron – a negatively charged particle that travels around the nucleus of an atom.

element – a pure substance made up of a single type of atom.

F

flammable – capable of being easily ignited.

G

gas – a state of matter where the particles do not touch each other.

group – a vertical column on the periodic table.

H

half-life – the time required for half the atoms in an isotope to change.

I

ionic bond – chemical link between atoms caused by electrostatic force between opposite charged ions.

isotope – an atom with the same number of protons and electrons, but a different number of neutrons.

L

liquid – a state of matter with a definite volume but not a definite shape.

M

malleable – able to be shaped or molded.

mass – the amount of matter a substance contains.

melting point – temperature at which a solid becomes a liquid.

mole – a unit of chemical mass equal to 6.022×10^{23} molecules or atoms.

N

neutron – a particle without electrical charge found in the atomic nucleus.

nucleus – the positively charged centre of an atom, made from protons and neutrons.

P

period – a horizontal row of the periodic table.

periodic table – the arrangement of elements by increasing atomic number.

pH – measure of the hydrogen ion concentration, reflecting how acidic or basic a solution is.

proton – a particle with a positive electrical charge found in the atomic nucleus.

R

radiation – the transfer of energy through waves, or moving particles.

radioactivity – the emission of radiation when atoms are broken apart.

reactant – a molecule involved in a chemical reaction.

reaction – a chemical change that forms new substances.

room temperature – a temperature that is comfortable for humans, generally around 20°C.

S

solid – a state of matter with a definitive shape and volume.

solution – a mixture of two or more substances.

spectroscopy – the study of light split into colours to determine the chemical composition of objects.

spectrum – the range of colours of electromagnetic radiation emitted by an object.

T

theory – a well-established set of scientific principles that explain a phenomenom.

U

unit – a standard of measurement.

V

vacuum – a volume containing little or no matter.

vapour – a condensable gas.

volume – the space occupied by a solid, liquid, or gas.

Y

yoctosecond – one yoctosecond is a trillionth of a trillionth of a second).

INDEX

Fans of The Extraordinary Elements
will also love these books:

The SPEED of STARLIGHT

A VISUAL EXPLORATION OF PHYSICS, SOUND, LIGHT, AND SPACE

Hardback: 9781787410749
Paperback: 9781787417229

The LANGUAGE of the UNIVERSE

A VISUAL EXPLORATION OF MATHEMATICS

Hardback: 9781787414075
Paperback: 9781787417878